T0318849

BORE HOLE
JOE MELLEN

This expanded edition published by Strange Attractor Press 2015.
© Joe Mellen 1970 / 2015.
2nd printing 2016.
Print on demand edition 2023.

First edition published by Joe Mellen 1970.
ISBN: 978-1-907222-39-9

Strange Attractor Press
BM SAP, London, WC1N 3XX, UK
www.strangeattractor.co.uk

Distributed by The MIT Press, Cambridge, Massachusetts.
And London, England.

CONTENTS

INTRODUCTION
Mike Jay

"This is the story of how I came to drill a hole in my head to get permanently high." Joey Mellen's memoir of his self-trepanation, memorably encapsulated in its opening sentence, has achieved a legendary status that reaches far beyond the 500 long-vanished copies he printed in 1970. It has been hailed as the blueprint for the next step in human evolution, denounced as a tragic example of the dangers of drug experimentation, and retold endlessly as an irresistible anecdote of high craziness. It has become the *ne plus ultra* of consciousness expansion, the extreme high water mark of the psychedelic sixties.

Yet with half a century of hindsight it becomes possible to view it as part of an older and more venerable tradition. In 1784 Immanuel Kant announced that the motto of the Enlightenment would be *sapere aude* – 'dare to know'. Nothing should be accepted on authority; everything should be put to the test. By this time many pioneers of the new sciences had already decided that personal experiment was the royal road to truth. In 1767 the famous surgeon Sir John Hunter allegedly investigated venereal disease by injecting the pus of an infected patient into his own penis. In 1780 the great physiologist Lazzaro Spallanzani discovered the existence of gastric juices by swallowing and regurgitating linen bags. Bold and self-sacrificing experiments form a continuous thread through medical science to the present day. The distinguished biologist JBS Haldane, after a lifetime of self-experimentation, insisted in 1971 – just as *Bore Hole* was first circulating – that he saw no scientific or ethical justification for performing experiments on any human or animal which he could equally well perform on himself. Even in our own risk-averse century, Barry Marshall won global acclaim, and the 2005 Nobel Prize for medicine, by infecting himself with the *Heliobacter pylorum* bacterium to demonstrate that it caused gastric ulcers.

Within this long and heroic tradition, there is one particular field where self-experimentation has always been uniquely valuable: the study of consciousness. Blood pressure, muscle contractions or hormone levels can be measured objectively, but states of consciousness are only accessible to the subject who experiences them. The first systematic experiments of this kind were conducted in 1799 by the young chemist Humphry Davy. Inhaling the newly discovered gas nitrous oxide, he was astonished to find himself projected into an inner world of dazzling sensations, insights and ideas. He enlisted his friends and colleagues, who included the romantic poets Coleridge and Southey, to set about mapping this new continent of the mind.

Davy's fearless self-experiments, during which he inhaled massive doses of nitrous and explored toxic gases almost to the point of death, launched a glittering career that saw him become Sir Humphry, President of the Royal Society and the great scientific genius of his generation. He was the living embodiment of sapere aude, the commitment to discovery that science would henceforth demand of its practitioners. His work set the template for a century and more of research on consciousness-altering drugs by the likes of Sigmund Freud, William James, Walter Benjamin and eventually Aldous Huxley – which is where Mellen came in. Reading Huxley's *Doors of Perception* as a teenager in 1959 introduced him to the idea of expanded consciousness; he sought out mescaline and then LSD, which he first encountered in Ibiza in the summer of 1965, courtesy of a Dutch medical student named Bart Huges. As well as a supply of privately manufactured acid from Amsterdam, Bart brought news of a mechanism he had discovered in the brain: if the blood supply to the capillaries that fed it was increased, it was able to operate at a higher capacity than normal. For Bart, this was already more than a theory: he was its walking proof. Earlier that year he had drilled a hole in his head.

Mellen's first acid experience was life-changing: he gave up his sixty-a-day cigarette habit on the spot and began to trip continually, all the while testing Bart's assertion that, in combination with sugar and Vitamin C, the radically expanded consciousness offered by LSD could be controlled and harnessed to expand the range of human possibility. He developed boundless energy and preternaturally enhanced senses, and began to consider Bart's proposition that it was possible to convert this condition from a temporary into a permanent one.

Trepanation is perhaps the oldest known surgical procedure in human history, and among the most widespread. Trepanned skulls thousands of years old have been found, often in large numbers, across both the Old World and the New. In the ancient cultures of the Americas the procedure was carried out with a sharp stone or curved knife; bone regrowth around the hole frequently shows that its subjects, or victims, lived on for many years. Its purposes in prehistoric cultures can only be guessed at: they might have included medical or psychotherapeutic interventions, initiation, punishment, a mark of distinction or a technique for divine communication.

In Europe trepanned skulls date back at least five thousand years, but the historical record begins with the Hippocratic writings of classical Greece. By the Renaissance a specialist instrument, the trephine, was well established in surgery: a hand drill surrounded by a set of teeth to grip the section of skull to be removed, such as Mellen used for his abortive first attempts. The uses of trepanation in early medicine are hard to translate into modern terms: "releasing evil spirits" or "cutting out the stone of folly" might be interpreted as relieving anything from epilepsy to migraine to psychosis. It is still practiced today, mostly for relieving intracranial pressure after head wounds, but the removed section of skull is typically replaced. Its history is extensive and full of interest, but it lacks any detailed first-person description of its effects on consciousness.

Mellen's unblinking account of his self-experiments is the book's claim to fame, but the subsequent story is equally compelling and in some ways more surprising, at least for the author. Having successfully elevated his consciousness, he was amazed to discover that trepanation was, in his wry understatement, "not everybody's cup of tea". In an era when the gulf between hip and straight was unbridgeable, the fact that he had taken drugs, let alone trepanned himself, automatically disqualified him from being taken seriously by the media and the wider public. Yet even among the countercultural vanguard, his discovery was received as only one revelation among many. Everyone had their own theory to push or spiritual quest to pursue; few seemed able to grasp that he had made a fundamental discovery, and that all they needed to do was what he had already done.

In the present-day reflections included in this volume Mellen considers all this with admirable honesty, detailing its consequences for Bart Huges and offering a considered assessment, forty-five years on, of life with a hole in the head. It seems likely that his testimony will remain unique. In our age of ethics committees and randomised control protocols, it is hard to imagine how his experiment could ever be officially repeated or corroborated. Clinical trials with LSD are slowly resuming after the cultural panic that shut them down a generation ago (thanks in no small part to the work of Mellen's former wife Amanda Feilding and her Beckley Foundation), but trepanation seems destined to remain what it has been ever since the sixties: the forbidden experiment, the epitome of too far.

Was the experiment worthwhile? There are only two ways to find out: trepan yourself, or read this book.

FOREWORD
Joe Mellen

I wrote the main part of this book in 1970. Most of the events I describe took place in the sixties, which were fresh in my memory. It was a decade that changed a lot of things. The sixties were my twenties, that period when, if one doesn't already know, one tries to decide where one is going in life. My life changed completely. After a conventional upbringing, the first joint I smoked set me off in the opposite direction. As Bob Marley said, "when you smoke the herb, it reveals you to yourself." My values were radically reversed. In retrospect I can now see that my experience was in fact typical of many in my generation. The beatniks were followed by the hippies, from pot to acid.

In fact the sixties were a watershed in more ways than one. In England there was a social revolution, with the old class system, which had endured for centuries, finally dissolving in the melting pot. In music, art, literature, fashion, theatre and film all the old barriers were stormed and the slaves poured into the streets in a joyous carnival of dancing and derring-do. There were many contributing causes to this great upheaval. It was a reaction to the austerity of the post-war years of the forties and fifties, the beginning of the surge in income that reached from the top down to the teenagers in the clubs with their record collections, books, clothes and world travel. Of course there was the pill. There was a massive levelling in the age of the National Health Service, state education, the grammar schools, the expansion of universities. There was television, Top Twenty, Kitchen Sink Drama, Nuclear Disarmament protests, Vietnam, the growth of Feminism etc etc.

Socialism had won the argument. Even the Tory party believed in equal opportunity.

But perhaps the greatest catalyst of change, at least among the young, was the use of psychedelic drugs, which endowed the peace and love movement with a religious, though not necessarily theistic, feeling that united the idealistic youth of the world in non-violent rebellion against the materialistic values of the old order, the repression and corruption of the corporate state and the military industrial complex that grabbed and kept both political and economic power for its own ends, to perpetuate its hold over the masses. The communist and capitalist systems were in many respects mirror images of each other, bureaucracies with opposing ideologies that cast each other as the villains (though it must be said that the individual enjoyed far greater freedom under our democratic capitalist system – I would have been locked up long ago in the Soviet Union and would never have been able to propagate the ideas in this book!). One thing that united them, however, was "The War on Drugs". Why they minded, and still mind, so much what people do to change their own consciousness is a hard question to answer. They obviously feel threatened, but why? Is it the independent thinking that the drugs engender?

Whatever the system of government, the inevitable problem is that the governors acquire a vested interest in staying in power. Skulduggery facilitates this aim. To achieve the Platonic ideal of a disinterested elite bearing the responsibility of governing on behalf of the people as a whole requires a degree of enlightenment that, in my opinion, can only come with the heightened consciousness psychedelic drugs make possible. Nobody truly enlightened WANTS to govern, but, in the interests of peace on earth, they may have to be persuaded to do so, at least for a limited time. As Jimi Hendrix said, "only when the power of love overcomes the love of power will the world know peace".

Unfortunately there is a great divide between those who take drugs (psychedelics in particular) and those who don't, and it is a gap that is almost unbridgeable. How can one explain to someone who hasn't taken them what the point is? The difficulty is that the advantage can't be explained; it has to be experienced. As Bart put it, "my problem is how to explain to the adult that he has too little blood in his brain to understand, if he has too little blood in his brain to understand that."

What this book, I hope, will do is give an answer to the question why do people want to take drugs, as they always have throughout history. This is an entirely new viewpoint, based on the discoveries of Bart Huges. He offers a physiological explanation of the effect of drug-taking and an evolutionary perspective on the reason for it. Everybody knows that the last thing anyone could possibly want, let alone need, is a hole in the head. You will also find that comfortable assumption challenged herein.

Joe Mellen,
London, August 2015.

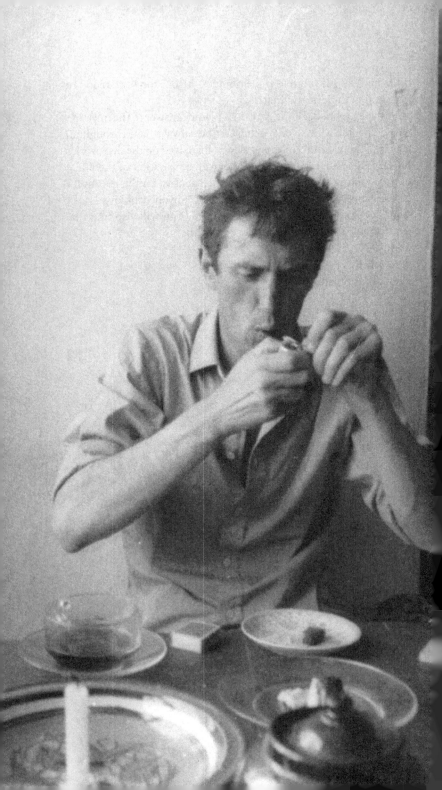

This is the story of how I came to drill a hole in my head to get permanently high.

I was born in a small Essex farmhouse a few days after the outbreak of war in September 1939. My father was American by birth, but after coming to Oxford University had taken British nationality and decided to live in England. He was the third of three sons and had a sister younger than him. He married my mother when he was thirty-one. She was ten years younger. Her family were "landed gentry" class, from Derbyshire. She was the youngest of three sisters, with a younger brother. When war was declared my father enlisted in the army and was posted from one camp to another. After ten months, with Hitler threatening invasion, my parents decided to send my older brother and me to America to stay with my father's family for the duration of the war. My mother took us over and left us with my grandmother and then returned to be with her husband.

My paternal grandfather had been a lawyer, like many of his ancestors, but had died before I was born. We lived with my grandmother, who presided over a large family of aunts, uncles, cousins etc, in New York in the winter and Maine, by the sea, for the summer months.

I learnt to walk and talk in America. I was there for three and a half years. I remember the tug boats on the river in New York and the yellow chequered taxicabs and I remember singing "Onward Christian Soldiers" with my grandmother after cleaning my teeth at night. Then it was decided that the threat of invasion by Hitler was past and we should be sent back to England. My brother went first, on the Queen Elizabeth battleship. On the crossing he fell down a scuttle and broke his collarbone. I stayed in New York and lost half my left thumb in a mincemeat machine, which curiosity led me to investigate while my grandmother was talking to the butcher. Two months later I was on the Atlantic in an old tramp steamer carrying one Hurricane fighter plane and an anti-aircraft gun. Every day they practised firing the gun. The whole ship shook as it went off.

I was one of fourteen children in the charge of a nurse. In the daytime I was tethered to a deck seat with a lead just long enough for me to hold the railings along the ship's side. There I watched the sea coursing past and rolling away over the horizon. At night I slept in a cabin with one porthole. Through that I could see the surface of the sea only a foot or two below, and often it would present a view of underwater as the ship yawed into a valley and then shuddered as she strove to rise again up the mountain, and the waves broke all over her and swished past the ship's sides with measureless pressure which made the bolts creak in their nuts in the cream-painted steel girders alongside my bunk. One beautiful clear day a flotilla of destroyers sailed past us. Their steel gleamed in the sunlight and great manes of spray arched from the bows as they cut through the water. They looked like a pack of sea wolves out hunting. Then they were gone and there was nothing but water again.

Many memories of this sea voyage have remained with me, so it must have made a deep impression. That is not surprising, since not only was it extraordinary in itself, but it must also, of course, have been a psychological passage of the utmost significance to a four-year-old, alone on the vast ocean, in transit between the old and a new world.

Back in England I had some difficulty adjusting to this family of strangers that was my real family. I did not recognize my parents, and a younger brother had been born in the meantime. It took some time to settle in, but the knack, once learnt, remained with me and from then on I could quite easily become one of the family with other households. The first time I saw my father he was in uniform. He looked very grand. We were living in a large house owned by my mother's parents. Their other children and their offspring were also there much of the time. I spent most of my time with my older brother Danny. He had a bad temper and we had frequent fights, which I got the worst of, but I still wanted to go around with him. One day, just before lunch, I was on the lawn with my younger brother, William. He could stand but not walk. I called to him and he walked across the grass to me. After that he gradually came into my life.

We moved to a much smaller house, where the family was alone together for the first time. My father said you were not a horseman until you had had three falls. It was not long before I qualified. During the year we lived there, surrounded by bracken and forest, I was taken cub-hunting for the first time. We started very early in the morning. It was dark outside and we had eggs for breakfast in the kitchen. It was bitterly cold. At the end of the hunt I was in a race with another boy to get to the kill first and be "blooded" – that is to have the face smeared with the fox's blood from the brush (the tail which they cut off) and not wash it off for twenty-four hours. I was relieved to lose the race.

Just across the road from our house was a saw mill and Mr Robertson, the owner, had lost several fingers in accidents. One day Danny and I went over to see him and he appeared with a rag tied round the stump of a thumb which he had just cut off that morning. He didn't seem too concerned. I think he only had four complete fingers left by now. It made my loss of a mere half thumb seem small fry.

My relationship with my mother was, of course, complicated by the break in it during my infancy. From ten months old to the age of four I had lived in America. This meant that my identification with her was interrupted during its inception, and by the time I returned the foundations of my personality had been laid down. That primary mother identification, which would normally be the keystone in those foundations, must have been displaced onto another figure, or perhaps even more than one.

The main figure in my American sojourn was my grandmother, a straight-backed but spindly old lady with the unshakeable moral convictions typical of her New England upbringing. There was something of the Spartan in that type and her husband, my grandfather, had had the romantic childhood of a pioneer. His father had entered into partnership with a certain General Palmer to build the first railroad to Colorado Springs in the Rockies. He had moved out west, built a mansion in the forest and reared his children there. My great grandmother had befriended the local Indians and fed them in her house. My grandfather had travelled east on a stage coach to attend his boarding school, once being chased by hostile Indians, so legend has it. Unfortunately he died before I was born, so I never saw him.

My only memory of an actual incident with my grandmother is, as I said, of singing "Onward Christian Soldiers" with her after cleaning my teeth at night, and I think that this must be a compound rather than a single image, reinforced by daily repetition. However her benign presence hovers over and behind that whole episode of my life, perhaps the most formative of all, certainly the one with the deepest memories, which underlies my whole consciousness. My feeling about her is of great kindness. Her grey hair up above her head in a bun gave her an authoritative air, but she twinkled and smiled. The figure that most resembles her in my memory is the old lady in the Babar books.

On my return my mother was a distant object of desire more than a real cuddly mama. She had a new baby, who must have been approximately the age I was when we'd parted, and I was an awkward interceptor, about whom she must have had some slightly guilty feelings. With my older brother, Danny, she had of course bonded before she'd left us. He was the first-born, born when she was newly married and in the spring of love eternal, and of course she had adored him as is usual in such circumstances. It was the summer of 1936, the war was not yet a serious threat. Life was still set in that pre-war atmosphere of certainty about the natural order of things. By the time I was born Danny was two and a half years old. For two and a half years he had been the only flower on the garden, soaking up all the parental sunshine. It must have been bad enough having a rival brother born, but then, ten months later, to be abandoned by his mother must have been deeply traumatic for him, and indeed it was. His upbringing was seriously disturbed.

The situation at the time of my birth was totally different. I arrived as war was declared. I can only have been an inconvenience. My mother breast-fed me but, on her own admission, never really bonded with me. Everything was in flux, uncertainty reigned. England was expecting invasion by Hitler. My mother was desperately in love with my father and wanted to be with him, come what may. The option of dumping the boys on granny in America was too tempting to resist. I have no definite judgement to make on the decision. I can understand it. It happened, so that's that. Some people say they can't imagine how a mother could do such a thing. Why didn't she stay with you, they say. How could she give her babies away? No doubt such arguments were raging in my mother's head at the time and no doubt they still resound dully deep in her memory. Deep down inside me I have a certain independence, which I can only attribute to this split in my mother figure identification and I think this led me into the self-contained world of books.

I have no memory of an intimate, cuddling relationship with my actual mother. I thought she was beautiful and I loved her and wanted to please her. I did this by being, relatively, successful at school. I was the most successful of the three brothers and in this way I gained her approval. Especially after my father died, when I was the eldest son at home, I enjoyed talking about serious things with her. She was not well educated herself. It was not considered necessary in those days for a woman. The important thing was to be attractive and accomplished in the arts of running a country house, so as to catch a worthy man to raise a family with. Gardening and antiques were her main areas of expertise. She regretted not having gone to university and pursued education beyond the elementary. She was a thinker. She enjoyed discussing the deeper questions of life.

In a way my relationship with her was somewhat similar to that with my American grandmother, in that she was at a remove from me all the time. She was also of the same determined conviction on moral issues. In the early days, before boarding school, we had village girls looking after us and there was Nanny in the background. First there were Peggy and Doris, then there was one called Primrose and later came May Bang. She had eleven brothers, most of whom were in prison at any one time, "banged up" as they say! The presence of these girls preserved the distance between our mother and us. We met mainly at mealtimes and then maybe for a bit in the evening when my father was back from work, before going to bed.

My main feelings about my mother were of her absolute fairness and integrity. She was sure of her values and true to them. If she said yes it meant yes, and no meant no. You could count on that. I suppose you could say that our relationship was one based on mutual admiration rather than love. The love, at least on her side, was conditional, but more of that later.

Because my infancy was for the most part as a younger brother, trying to keep up with the older one and not quite succeeding, it became habitual for me to pretend to be less afraid than I really was and to say I could do what I really couldn't. Speech became my speciality. At five I became an avid reader, and between five and eight I consumed volumes of words. I could lose myself in the fantasy world of King Arthur, Robin Hood and all the other heroes of children's classics. I remember once sitting reading a book with my back against a fireguard just in front of an electric fire. My reverie was interrupted by Nanny bursting into the room in alarm. The room was full of smoke and the back of my sweater was charred black, like burnt toast. I hadn't noticed a thing.

Nanny was an old girl whose face was whiskery, or perhaps wispy would be a better word. It was, if not covered, at least sprinkled with long wispy grey hairs, which couldn't quite be described as a beard. I was very fond of Nanny, but I didn't like her goodnight kisses because of the whiskers. She had a tiny pewter teapot which held enough for one cup and she was back and forth between nursery and kitchen all day long, brewing up.

We moved again, for the last time, to settle in a rambling old Tudor farmhouse with a large garden. My father had got a well-paid job as a stockbroker in the City of London, and he commuted by train. He had very little capital and it was his intention to live well and send his children to the best schools. At that time the public school system was considered to give the best education and that meant paying high fees. His income as a stockbroker enabled him to carry out his intentions. Apart from that he was not very satisfied with the job, feeling it to be unproductive. He would rather have been a farmer. In the summer he used to get up at five in the morning and go out riding on his cob, Gunner, before breakfast, then change into a suit and drive to the station.

Danny was very keen on farming. He was out all day on the tractors. To me he behaved as if he was infinitely superior and more grown up, out doing a full day's work. Aged eight, he once swaggered into the house and proclaimed, "phew, first hot dinner of the week!" as he tucked into lunch. I enjoyed riding the tractors for a bit, but got bored when I realised that they just went back and forth doing the same thing all the time.

Soon after we arrived at our new house, when he was eight, Danny was sent to boarding school. I thought he was incredibly brave, going off on his own like that, and felt very sorry for him. His leaving brought our close relationship to an end. By the time he came back for the holidays, three months later, I had forged a new relationship with William, in which I was now the older brother, a role I much preferred. My friendship with William lasted for the rest of my childhood. Later on we both had dogs, he a large black Labrador and me a small white terrier. The terrier was the tyrant.

Our house was just outside the village. We got to know the children in the village, the Reynoldses, the Trickers, the Barkers, the Bakers and the Monkses. There were only a few main families, all interrelated by marriage, as was common in villages at that time. Nearly all the men worked as labourers on the local farms. The Trickers had thirteen children. My first girlfriend was the vicar's daughter. When I was eight it was my turn to go to boarding school. This put a rift between "us" and "them" which was never firmly bridged again. I was mad about cricket; they were not. I learnt Latin and all my friends spoke posh. Back at home the village and the village children's games seemed rather slow and boring. Though we knew each other by sight and name, the great social divide kept us apart. For friends we looked to the neighbouring families of our own class. There were several families within bicycling or riding distance. For a number of years a family lived in the farm next door with two daughters, Venetia and Ginny, one my age and the other William's. They became our most constant playmates. I remember my first sexual frisson hiding in a cupboard in the dark with Ginny. During my first year at boarding school my sister Susan was born. My father was delighted to have a little girl at last.

At one time my father must have been making quite a bit, because we had a cook and a butler, who lived in the back part of the house, beyond the kitchen, which had been blocked off from the rest of the house and turned into the servants' quarters. There was a succession of these husband and wife teams, but the longest lasting were the Goddards. Goddard, as my mother and father called him (Mr Goddard to the children) was totally bald. Apparently it had been caused by shell shock in the war. As a result he always wore a brown trilby when he went out. At various times we had crazes for different sweets and one of these was for sherbert fizzes, with that delicious frothing of the foam crystals in the mouth.

Goddard used to do the shopping in Dunmow and William and I liked to go too, partly for the fun of it but also I suspect for the possibilities it offered of getting sweets. We sat in the back seat and on one particular occasion we were in the throes of sherbert addiction. As we jogged along in the back of the car with Goddard's hairless neck rising into his trilby in front of us, we couldn't resist sprinkling sherbert powder onto the rim of the hat. To do this without him noticing took a lot of cunning and we succeeded admirably, the rim containing a thin layer of white by the time we got to Luckins, the grocers. Goddard never took his hat off when he was out. He only did that when he got home. The anticipation of this great event had us in a state of suppressed laughter and excitement all the way home, which was finally released when he did take it off and a cloud of white powder fell to earth via his shoulder and sleeve.

On another occasion Danny drove a tractor from a gate in one field across the road to another field through a facing gate and, as luck would have it, a police car happened to drive by at that precise moment. In those days a police car on those pretty empty country roads was a very rare sight and I suppose the sight of an eleven-year-old boy driving a tractor was equally rare for the police. At any rate it provided them with an incident and the upshot was that my father lost his driving license for a year, since he was considered responsible, even though he was at work in his office in London and had nothing whatsoever to do with it. It was the farmer who had let Danny drive the tractor.

The consequence of this was that Goddard had to drive my father to the station every morning and collect him in the evening. He had an unfortunate and very irritating mannerism of continually cocking his wrist, as it were, on the steering wheel

as he drove along. The white cuff of his shirt inched up out of the sleeve of his jacket as his elbow rose in the air in front of my father in the passenger seat. It used to drive my father mad and I remember him raging about it when he got home and was having a Martini.

At school Danny was Mellen major and I was Mellen minor. He was two and a half years older than me, which meant seven or eight terms' superiority. To a third-termer a new boy is so small he is almost invisible, so obviously one didn't mix with boys who had been there seven terms longer. He had his friends, I had mine. From the start I was good at work and was always among the top few. We were given plus marks for good work and minus marks for bad results or bad behaviour. In the order of merit which was published periodically my high minus score for bad behaviour always kept me from top place, though few got higher plus scores over the term. If your balance was a surplus of minus over plus it was written in red, as overdrawn bank accounts were in those days. That was never my fate, but Charlie DuCane, who was none too bright academically and very naughty, almost invariably had a huge overdraft!

The school, Ludgrove, was a prep school for Eton. The great majority of the boys went on there. It was a large Victorian country house set in its own grounds, which must have covered fifty acres or more. There were extensive playing fields and long paths that led between them and other areas, fringed with great clumps of rhododendrons into which you could dive and disappear playing hide and seek games. There was a pond in a wood, also surrounded by rhododendrons, in which we built dens for our scout troops – mine was the Otters – and made camp fires on which we cooked twist, dough rolled out into lengths and twisted around a stick to be toasted over the red hot embers.

The drive leading to the main road was about half a mile long and a couple of miles away lay the little town of Wokingham. Once or twice a term we would be taken out by our parents, always on a Sunday. The place to go was the Terrace Café, which served the most delicious Welsh rarebit. One time four of us decided to break bounds and go there by ourselves. We had saved up enough pocket money for Welsh rarebits each and it all went perfectly according to plan. At one point we had to leap into a ditch and hide when we saw a master's car coming down the drive, but we weren't spotted and the delicacy had never tasted so good after the long walk and the frisson of breaking the law. Unfortunately on the return journey we were five minutes late and the door was locked. We had to try and get in through the woodwork room and were caught at the last minute. The punishment was to be caned.

In a way boarding school is a prison and the masters are more than just teachers, they are the authorities. They make and enforce the rules. In a situation where you can be punished for possession of a water pistol, you can imagine how great it was raiding dormitories and having water pistol battles. If it could be fun, prohibit it, seemed to be the general idea behind the legislation. The worst punishment was caning. The next in severity to caning, was called "drill". It involved running round the gym with a first world war blunderbuss held above the head. One got a stitch and the sergeant-major bawled at one to keep going.

On Guy Fawkes night we burnt effigies of the Labour ministers on bonfires. The Attlee government was in power at the time. The headmaster, a staunch conservative, like ninety nine percent of the parents I'm sure, had been captain of the Yorkshire cricket team and almost played for England, so the story went. The cricket team was his pride and joy. Once, after the first eleven lost a match against weak opponents, he forbade the members of the team their usual privilege of a swim after the game and cancelled the school film that week.

On the whole I enjoyed myself. We were there for thirty-six weeks in the year, so that was the best policy. The authorities were just the fuzz on the peach. I liked games: cricket, football, fives and squash, and I was good at work. I read a lot of books, the Just William and Biggles books, Captain Hornblower, the Swallows and Amazons, Sherlock Holmes, *Treasure Island* and *Kidnapped*, the heart-breaking *Black Beauty* etc. For a time I had a passion for Agatha Christie murder mysteries and also Peter Cheyney, with his wise-cracking detectives, Lemmy Caution and Slim Callaghan. I remember Slim's line "I'm gonna knock seventeen different kinds of hell outta that guy" and Lemmy's observation after being roughed up himself, "I'm holding a conference with myself to see whether I'm standing on my right ear or my left elbow". After that my reading developed into the study of cricket literature.

To those who do not understand the game of cricket it is hard to see what it is all about. At the highest level a game lasts for five days and every ball bowled and the batsman's playing of it is recorded in the score book. Owing to the great length of the game there is much theorizing over strategy and tactics. The nature of the grass wicket changes as the conditions change. Experience counts for much and knowledge is as important as skill. The captain is like the commander of the army in battle. He directs operations and does the thinking. The literature on the game is copious, abounding with legendary feats that have the scores to validify them. I was hooked on the narrative style from all the adventure stories I had read. Cricket stories were about real events and there to reinforce the reality was a great mass of facts and figures to research in *Wisden*, the cricketer's almanack. Published yearly, it is a thick tome containing the results and statistics of all first class games played during the year in all the cricket-playing countries, as well as all the records of every kind since way back in the last century. By thirteen I was a walking *Wisden*. It was a satisfying study because I knew the world of cricket and could identify with every action described, whereas history always seemed more like the story books, about kings and queens and events I was unfamiliar with. If there had been an exam in cricket literature I would have been top every time.

Outside the window of the top form there was a woodpecker who appeared every morning. We called him Guzzle. He was a regular happening for a long time and then one day he was gone, never to return. I wrote a poem called "Lament for Guzzle". It was considered so good that it was stuck up on the school notice board. I always had a facility for rhyming and Latin verse was my best subject.

The first year I was at this school I was put against an older boy in the school boxing competitions. He was two feet taller than me and had only to keep me at arm's length to render my blows ineffective. I lost the fight. After that I became very good at boxing and didn't lose another fight at that school. I continued boxing right through to university, where I ended up captain of the team.

At home in the holidays it was quite a different scene. The most regular happening was taking the dogs out hunting with William. Every day we took them out across the fields and through the woods. We knew all the countryside around the house up to a distance of three miles or more and would change our beat frequently. One summer, before myxomatosis, the dogs caught forty-six rabbits in six weeks (not to mention rats). We gutted and skinned the rabbits and then cooked them, mainly for the dogs. Later William took up riding a pony and my major preoccupation became girlfriends. All my girlfriends were crazy about horses. I had given up riding when I went to boarding school and now only rode a bike. It was not uncommon for me to ride five or six miles to spend the day with Annabella, while she would ride her pony over to me.

I loved my father. He was such fun to be with. He was up early in the morning and was gone to the station before we got up, but often of a summer's evening William and I would set off down the road to Elsenham to meet him on his way back. We would walk a mile or two and then flag him down when we saw the car coming. On the way home he would tell us jokes and sing songs. "Mares eat oats and Does eat oats and little Lambs eat ivy" was a favourite. He could fart at will too, an enviable talent which was also great entertainment. Sometimes he would do it while carving the joint on Sunday. That was especially delightful because my mother disapproved and there was the extra pleasure of conspiratorial laughter. Looking back, I see the identification with my father as the most positive influence on my life.

There were a lot of upper middle class children's parties. I wore a dinner jacket from thirteen onwards and did the Eightsome reel, Petronella and Dashing White Sergeant. I remember the fever of love for one girl and then another, the agony of parting, and waiting. The dance floor was the one area where bodily contact was expected and many's the romance that's taken wing from smooching cheek to cheek at late night teenage parties in the dark.

I went to Eton when I was thirteen. From the country house

atmosphere of prep school to the hurly burly of Etonian town life was a big change. There one was, back at the bottom of the pile, a new boy again. Eton consists of about thirty separate houses in a town, with school buildings and playing fields all around. Each boy had his own room, which was a big step up from dormitory life. In each house there were about forty boys.

When I was fourteen my father died. I was given the news by my housemaster, though I had a premonition of it when someone told me he wanted to see me at an unusual time. I went to his study and he gave me the news. He told me that Nancy Tennant, a family friend, was coming to collect me and take me home. I kept a straight face in front of my housemaster, John Herbert, a kind man with a nicotine-stained moustache, but when I got back to my room I flung myself onto the bed and collapsed in floods of tears. I had a series of what I can only call hallucinations. Flashes of my father kept appearing to me, laughing with his red spotted handkerchief round his neck, carving the joint, cutting the branch off a tree, as real as if he was there. Then the reality broke in again and I cried until it felt as if my eyes were inside out.

My father had been ill for two years or more. The doctors didn't know what was wrong. They had operated twice. He had high blood pressure, which created complications in his kidneys. I always suspected that this was caused by the extreme exertion of rowing. At Oxford he had stroked the eight for two years and at the end of the boat race one year the stitches from his recent appendectomy had burst. He was much lighter than the rest of the crew, but made up for the weight deficiency with abnormal will power and determination. However my youthful diagnosis was almost certainly wrong. I remember he was a salt addict. He used masses of salt with his food and loved things like "Gentleman's Relish", an incredibly salty anchovy paste. It was 1953 and in those days dialysis machines were a brand new invention. A group of his friends clubbed together to buy one for the hospital. It arrived the day after he died. My mother was in the room when he died in his sleep. After the funeral I went back to school, where my friends soon made me feel at home again. He was buried in a grave abutting the wall between our garden and the churchyard.

My mother never really recovered. She couldn't really talk

about my father. At the mention of his name she would burst into tears and leave the room, so we soon learnt not to do that. It was as if part of her died too. Though I knew that there were offers, she never considered marrying again. She bottled up her feelings with a stiff upper lip, put a brave face on and carried on suffering. Besides the depressed atmosphere which followed my father's death, the sudden drop in income reduced our financial circumstances considerably. No more cook and butler. To keep the house she went into rearing pigs. The gardener became pig-keeper too. We had about sixty pigs at a time. They rooted around in the orchard, turning the grass to mud. I used to muck them out as one of my holiday jobs, not paid but expected as a contribution to the family welfare.

Gradually the new regime established itself. The one who suffered most from it was my sister. She had been only six when my father died. Although she had been the apple of his eye and obviously adored him, she has no memory of him. At the time I had little to do with her. As a teenager I was on the hunt for girlfriends. Social life took up most of my time. Susan was always on a pony. There was one interest we shared however, and that was music. She took piano lessons and I played a banjo ukulele. I wrote a song to sing with her. The refrain went: "At the rainbow's end there's a pot of gold, maybe I'll find it when I get old, but for now I just can't lose the memory of you". The tune and rhythm were none too loosely based on a huge hit at the time, Paul Anka's "Diana". Later in life Susan became a songwriter and when she wrote a number one worldwide hit, called "Nine to Five" and sung by Sheena Easton, she did indeed hit the jackpot. She is now the closest to me of all my family. For several years, before she went to boarding school at the age of eleven, she bore the brunt of my mother's depression, being her sole companion for all the time that William and I were at school. Danny by now had left home and was living in Ireland with our cousins, the sons of my mother's oldest sister, who lived in Mayo. Nick, the older son, trained point-to-pointers and had a small lobster fleet. The life was outdoor, hard-drinking and just what Danny liked. He had a great time there and it was the first step into his career as a steeplechase jockey.

My mother's attitude was a mixture of bravery and bitterness.

She felt robbed by life of a happiness that she could never regain. She had been a romantic; now she became a stoic. She cut herself off from the world of emotion and got on with the business of enduring and surviving. She immersed herself in the practicalities of keeping the house running, entertaining the children, feeding the animals, gardening, doing a bit of antiquing. Gradually, as the tragedy receded, her spirits got lighter, but there was always the feeling that she was a martyr, sacrificing happiness for duty, her reward to follow in heaven. "Isn't Bridget wonderful!" all her friends would say, and perhaps this was her reward on earth. Her mood with the children was strict, suffering foolishness badly, tolerant as long as we stayed within the rules, didn't bring our dirty boots into the main part of the house, that sort of thing. One thing I will say for her though; she was always extremely accommodating where my romances were concerned. She ferried me to and fro from parties and if I had a party at home would make herself scarce, leave me alone with my friends, whether plural or singular, with the run of the gramophone and drawing room. I got on really well with her for the most part and liked being the oldest male in the house.

I enjoyed my time at Eton. Once I had got used to the size of it and could find my way around there was so much to do. We had a lot of freedom. Every other day there was no work in the afternoons, only games, and after the games were finished you could go anywhere you wanted in the extensive grounds. We were allowed to cross over the bridge to Windsor and one of the essential qualifications to become a real Etonian was to do the long walk, which was to the statue of George the Third in Windsor Great Park, down a very long straight road from the castle. Once when I was doing it a car came past with the Royal Family in and they all waved to us. Ordinary cars weren't allowed down that road.

Public schools enjoy, or at least have, a reputation for rampant homosexuality. This is not altogether surprising, since, at least in those days, there were no girls there and in those early pubic years the instinct does tend to dominate one's life. Willy nilly one is forced into the company of other boys. The activities we indulged in were no more than flushed gropings, "fiddling" as it was called. We used to handle each other's genitals, with all the excitement that comes from the forbidden increasing the sensual pleasure. Our group spread over three different houses and we used to meet in secret places. Eventually we were caught at it. Because there were so many of us, about fifteen in all, we couldn't be sacked. It would have caused too great a scandal. So we were beaten instead and that put an end to that.

Besides the slightly ridiculous games that were peculiar to Eton, the field game and the wall game, all sorts of other games were played. In winter we played football and rugby. There were rows of fives courts, squash and rackets courts and a big gym in which I spent a lot of my time, not only boxing, but fencing and doing gymnastics, which I was quite good at too. I sang in the Lower Chapel choir, won a singing competition, took part in the school play and joined various societies, which got one out of the house in the evenings to attend lectures or concerts or whatever the activity might be, play-reading or debating for example. One such outing was a most memorable event.

There was a concert in School Hall. A famous pianist, Moisevitsch by name, was to give a recital for the Music Society. Some old boys from the house next to School Hall had come down for the day and they stationed themselves on the roof of the adjacent house. They had equipped themselves with torches and mirrors. When the maestro had taken his seat the hall was hushed. At that moment two spots of light appeared on the walls and played around a bit before coming to rest on the keyboard. As the hands began to move over the keys, so the spots of light followed them, occasionally doing a little bit of embroidery over the polished wood for good measure. It was incredibly funny and the smothered giggles grew louder and louder until they burst the banks of decorum. Finally the headmaster stood up and brought the concert to a halt.

The next day word was sent to every house that two scapegoats from each were to be beaten as an example that such behaviour could not be tolerated. I had gone with a friend from my house, Martin Summers, who later became one of the owners of the Lefevre Gallery in Bruton Street, London's leading impressionist gallery, and we were the only two junior members of the house there, not that juniors had made any more noise than the older boys, but they always get picked on in such situations. Anyway, it so happened that both Martin and I were also out on that night at other society meetings, so we weren't there after supper at the traditional beating time. The following day the headmaster sent round to find out if any of the intended scapegoats had slipped through the net. It had been decided that an even more drastic example should be made, pop-tanning.

Pop was the self-elected society of senior boys of outstanding ability or merit of some other form, which acted as sort of school prefects. Certain boys, such as the captain of the school, the captain of cricket, the field game, the eight and so on, were ex officio members. The rest were elected by the other members. They were la crème de la crème and they knew it. They wore fancy waistcoats, spongebag trousers, stick-up collars and white bow ties. Pop-tanning was the most fearsome punishment, the cane that was used being especially thick and containing knots in the wood at regular intervals on its length.

At nine o'clock in the morning Martin and I received fagnotes telling us to come to Pop Room at two thirty. Fagnotes were a system of communication, by which older boys in authority could send messages to each other or anybody else, having them delivered by fags, or junior boys, whom they summoned by standing and shouting "Boy!" at the tops of their voices in a particular cadence, at the sound of which all junior boys had to run to the source of the noise, the last one to get there being deputed to perform the task. In each house there was a letter rack on the notice board into which these notes, folded in a characteristic way, could be inserted.

The receipt of these notes sent shivers of fear through us, which we had to endure for the whole morning and through lunch before the appointed hour arrived. Once there we were kept waiting outside for some time before being summoned in. The members of Pop were assembled, sitting on chairs placed on top of tables around the walls of the room, so that they looked down on us like gods from a great height. We were given a lecture and told to wait outside. Then I was called in first. I was told to place my head under the lip of the table at the end of the room, while the president of Pop prepared to beat my taut buttocks. At the third stroke the cane broke and a titter of laughter spread through the room. I got up, thinking it was over, but was told to get down again. A new cane was produced and another two strokes administered, which were doubly painful due to the gap in time, which had allowed the previous ones to start smarting as the immediate numbness wore off. The only compensation for this blatant piece of injustice was that we were instant heroes for a few days, since pop-tanning was extremely rare and everyone wanted to hear about the experience. I remember the name of the president of Pop to this day and I vowed that if ever I came across him I would give something to remember me by!

When I think back to my days at Eton now it was in many ways idyllic. The screen memory, as it were, is of sauntering around, hands in pockets, or casually throwing a cricket ball to a friend on Dutchman's Plough to see how high and far one could throw it. There was a lot of sauntering going on. The world belonged to us. In atlases of the time vast areas of the world were coloured pink, the British Empire. Britain ruled the waves and we ruled Britain. Where was the battle of Waterloo won after all?

After leaving I didn't return to the school for many years, but once, perhaps twenty years later, as we were driving down the motorway past Windsor, Amanda (of whom more in due course), on a whim, suddenly suggested going to have a look at the school, which she had never been to. By a stroke of serendipity it happened to be the fourth of June, which is the big day when all parents come down and have picnics on Agars Plough with summer dresses and hats, strawberries and champagne, all leading up to the climax of the procession of boats on the river at sunset, followed by the fireworks. All of this only added to the impression of a world in a bubble. I took Amanda to Luxmoore's Garden, a small island, or eyot, in the Thames, reached by a narrow bridge. It is a very peaceful and secluded spot, with the mown grass reaching down to water under the willow trees. I had specialised in "Classics General". We were a small group of about fifteen. We did Latin, Greek and English literature. In the summer term, when the weather was good, we used to have lessons in Luxmoore's Garden. As I was showing Amanda where we used to sit and do our Latin construe, toes dabbling in the water, I looked up and caught a glimpse of College Chapel through the trees. How beautiful it was. I was struck by the realisation that in those days this was everyday normal life for me. Now I saw what an ivory tower it was.

My teens coincided with the arrival of rock and roll. You were allowed a radio in your room, a wireless as we called it then, but the only good music programme was Radio Luxembourg and reception was at best intermittent. It came and went, so you might hear one third of a song quite clearly and one third fighting with atmospheric interference in a shroud of crackle, while the remainder disappeared completely.

To listen to the latest records you had to frequent the record shops. There the top twenty list was displayed and you could listen through earphones in the cubicles. There was a good record shop just off the high street, down a little alley in a prefab hut. I got a crush on the girl behind the counter – well, she was more than a girl, she was a married woman in fact. We had a sort of totally platonic affair. It was all in the eyes. The hut was a pleasure dome, listening to the music in that high-tension state of calf love, the secret intimacy of our glances ratcheting it up to an almost unbearable erotic pitch. The nearest we ever got to real contact was holding hands as we went for a walk in Windsor Great Park.

I was extremely ignorant of the facts of life, though I did know that babies resulted from sexual intercourse. I never had the confidence to attempt the ultimate with one of my girlfriends. I wasn't even sure exactly what you did – I mean who was where, you know, which way round exactly … When I was seventeen I went with a prostitute in London on the way to or from school and then I knew it was as simple as I'd thought it must be. It was a loveless experience, but not without its humorous side. Fortified by a strong whisky, I strolled as nonchalantly as I could past the many girls in the Shepherd Market area, trying to spot one I liked the look of. I finally made up my mind to approach one of them. She led me upstairs to a small room. Shyly I confessed that it was my first time. It was a simple job for her. She produced a vibrator, something I'd never heard of let alone seen before, and expertly fitted a condom on before completing what must have been her quickest "trick" that day.

At eighteen I went up to Oxford. There was still national service at the time, but my call-up was deferred for three years. In the end it was abolished five days before my final exams. I had decided to go into the Navy. I had hated the Army section of the Corps at Eton, which had been compulsory for the first two or three years. It seemed to consist of nothing but square-bashing and cleaning kit, blancoing spats and belts, polishing boots and buckles and all that sort of bullshit. The sea seemed much more romantic. To go into the Navy I had to enlist in the RNVR and go on a training fortnight. I received instructions in the mail to turn up at 20.00 at Plymouth Docks to join my frigate.

My hair was rather long in those days, not hippy long, just a bit over my ears you know, but even that was uncommon in the late fifties. I had worked out that 20.00 hours meant 8pm and I was at the gate at five to eight. The sentry came to attention, saluted and said, "Good evening madam. What can I do for you?" It was not a good start. When I got on board I found that I was easily the last of the one hundred trainees, who were in the charge of fifty regulars. There were knowing looks passed between them, as if to say, "Oi, oi, this is the one we've been waiting for!"

Each trainee had a special duty assigned to him besides the general duties that everyone had, like swabbing the decks. It might be making the officers' beds, that sort of thing. Mine was "cleanin' out for'ard 'eads and bathrooms", which I found out meant the lavatories. There were six cubicles without doors. A single copy of the Daily Mirror provided the reading matter for the whole voyage of two weeks, being passed sheet by sheet from seat to seat. It was very choppy on the Irish Sea and the plumbing was pretty choppy too, the contents rising and falling with their own internal rhythm. After a week at sea we ran out of Jeyes Fluid, which had been my shelter in a storm.

By the time I arrived on board all the best places to sling a hammock had been taken. In fact there was only one place left and that was right up in the point of the bows, directly beneath the cable locker. The noise of the iron links of the cable rasping over the ship's side above my head every time we dropped or weighed anchor was absolutely deafening. Apart from that, sleeping in a hammock was very comfortable and life on the lower deck had its compensations, particularly the daily tot of rum.

Conversation, however, was severely restricted by the prohibition on three subjects: religion, politics and sex. That left sport and entertainment, music and films as the common currency. Pin-ups were allowed.

Towards the end of my first year I met Mish. This was what I had been waiting for. We fell head over heels in love with each other. A girl friend at home had told me that her best friend was going to a finishing school in Oxford and I ought to meet her because she was very attractive. When I did meet her I found out how right she was. The world took on a rainbow hue and I had never imagined such happiness. Luckily we lived only twenty five miles apart at home and, since I had the use of an old 1938 Morris Minor with a hood that leaked, this meant that we could be together most of the time. Mish was seventeen, two years younger than me. She was a virgin and wanted to stay that way until she was married. I would have preferred it otherwise, but since I was sure that she was going to marry me, I agreed to wait. It kept the passion at boiling point constantly. She was so sexy, Mish, and the sexiest thing of all was her voice, slightly husky, especially when laughing. I remember the first time we lay together in a field on a sunny day and with trembling fingers I undid her dress to reveal her bare breasts. The glory of that sight, the beauty of her body, the soft firmness of the English rose, this was what it was all about, the stuff of rhapsody. This was ecstasy, the real thing. All the stories were true, the clichés justified. We kissed for ever, on and on in an infinite trip through the bliss of being lost and found at the same time, in love with each other and the whole world, careless, perfect, first true teenage love.

Our romance began on New Year's Eve. In the summer Mish left Oxford to become a debutante and do the London season. I went to a hundred balls dressed in tails and drank and ate in great houses beneath glittering chandeliers. Our love survived until the autumn, when Mish went up to Scotland for yet more Highland balls. It was the first time we had spent more than two days apart in nine months. I was approaching my twentieth birthday and life without Mish was dull and lonely. I wrote long letters to Scotland and at first got long ones back. Then the letters back got shorter and the intervals between them longer. When I met the train at

King's Cross I knew something had happened. Mish was friendly but something was missing. Finally, in floods of tears, she told me she had fallen in love with someone else. My dream was shattered. At first I couldn't really believe it; then, as I had done at an earlier crisis in childhood, I withdrew into myself and took to reading.

It was now the field of religion that caught my interest. I read Aldous Huxley's *Perennial Philosophy*, then the *Doors of Perception*. That was my introduction to the world of expanded consciousness. Another influential book was called *Wisdom Madness and Folly; the Philosophy of a Lunatic*. I can't remember the name of the author, but he was a manic-depressive and the book was about the religious insight his madness afforded him. I had found the book in the shelves of a doctor's waiting room. I had been waiting for Serena, who lived near us in the country. I fancied Serena and had asked her out to dinner. She was staying in her father's house in Kensington Square. It was a large house and they had let off some rooms on the ground floor to a doctor. The servant who opened the door had told me to wait while she went upstairs to find Serena. While waiting I browsed through the bookshelves and came across this book. Serena took her time appearing, which enabled me to start reading it. I then borrowed it and took it home to finish.

Apart from reading and playing poker and going to parties my main activity at Oxford was boxing. In my second year I was made secretary of the boxing club, which involved writing to all the prospective opponents and arranging the bouts, booking the bus and that sort of thing, quite a lot of extra work. I explained this to my tutor, who excused me tutorials for the two winter terms. In my final years I was captain, so that workload passed to the new secretary. I was then in the position of choosing the team, in conjunction with Alf Gallie, the coach. One of the team I picked was a Texan who always carried his guitar with him. He was Kris Kristofferson, who later wrote such classic songs as 'Help Me Make It Through The Night' and 'Me and Bobby McGee', so memorably sung by Janis Joplin. I always remember one incident with Kris. We were in Jersey to fight the Channel Islands team. Kris's opponent had been a finalist in the Empire Games and was extremely classy. Kris took a hammering. He was knocked down about nine times and the referee finally stopped the fight just before the end of the third and last round. He had put up an incredibly brave fight against a far superior opponent. He came into the dressing room and said, "Sorry guys, guess I just ran out of gas!".

Work took a back seat. After the first two terms, when lectures had been essential every day for prelims, the routine was very laid back. We had a tutorial once a week, for which we had to write an essay. It was entirely up to us when and where we worked. In my second year, as I have explained I did virtually no work at all. The point of being at Oxford was not to get a degree. I attached no importance to that. The point was to have a good time in the company of intelligent young people, to think and drink. My father had been rusticated for doing no work. He hadn't got a degree, but he had been the first American ever to row for Oxford and in the twenties to be an Oxford rowing blue, especially stroke, was very glamorous. It was only in my last year that the degree assumed any importance at all and this was because, not having any idea what I wanted to do in life, but realizing that the real world was waiting outside the gates and that I was going to have to earn a living somehow, I began to give it some thought. My father's firm had been keeping a seat warm for one of his sons and, since I was the brightest, academically speaking, I was the chosen one. I had no great ambition to be a stockbroker in the City, but, since I had no great ambition for any other career either and I knew that at least it was very well paid, I had begun to think why not, faute de mieux. The normal procedure was for new members of the firm to buy a partnership, to put some money in the kitty, so to speak. Since they realised that this was something I couldn't do, they suggested that I take a chartered accountant's course and come with that qualification.

I discovered that this course lasted five years without a degree, but only three with one. Suddenly I saw the point of getting a degree. The only problem was that I was way behind with my work. Of the eight subjects I had only covered five. The other three were a blank. I had about four months before the exams. The urgency stimulated me to concentrate all my energies into the task. I looked up all the exam papers for the last six years and analysed the questions in each. Four essays were required for each paper. I reckoned that if I could prepare six for each subject I stood a sporting chance of getting by. I then worked fourteen hours a day for four months without a break. I started before breakfast. Every day I was the first one into the library and the last to leave. Then I would work in my room till midnight. It worked. I got an un-viva-ed third.

I was now an adult. The chartered accountant's course was the most boring thing I have ever done. Basically the articled clerks were slaves. We did the dog's body work all day long, ticking rows of figures in one ledger against rows of figures in another. The pay was ridiculously low, £400 per annum. Even in those days there was no way you could live on that. There was also a correspondence course to be done in our spare time. Half way through the three year course I took the intermediate exam and failed one paper out of six. I had to sit all six again six months later and this time I passed. This was real adulthood. The prospect of spending the rest of my life in a City office block filled me with dread. I was up all night, squeezing as much fun as possible into the time available, so I yawned my way through the days, surrounded by scurf-ridden senior clerks with halitosis. The only thing that lightened the gloom was the organising of an office competition of Battleships between the articled clerks. When we got bored with that we started another of the Word Game, seeing how many words of three or more letters you could get out of one of six or seven letters. When the senior clerk appeared the sheets of paper were hastily thrust under the desk, just like the Agatha Christie at school.

For two months I had a love affair with a pretty girl called Louisa, then that came to an end. I was living in the house of one of my Oxford friends in London. In that period I met Jane. She was very attractive and her mode of life was different. Most of her friends were eccentrics, homosexuals and petty criminals, in marked contrast to the ambassadorial elegance of her home life. One group were smoking pot, which was far out in those days. Jane tried to turn me on, but I resisted. I said I didn't want to get involved with drugs, though I was a non-stop drinker and tobacco smoker.

The time came to take the final exams. I had six weeks' study leave before them, which I intended to spend at home in the country. I sat down in front of a pile of books on estate duty, income tax and such subjects and a great resistance welled up inside me. What was I doing learning about those things? Did I want to know them? No, I didn't. Did I want to be a stockbroker? No. Did I want to be rich? Yes, but not that much. Even more I wanted to have a good time now, while I was young. I was reading Ouspensky's *In Search of the Miraculous*. I decided to read on for one more day and start my studying tomorrow. Tomorrow it was put off for another day. Then I started writing down my thoughts and I soon found that this was a great help in clarifying matters for me. Suddenly I felt as if there was so much to think about that all I wanted was to have all my time to spend thinking about it. Writing was the way to look at what I was thinking, to criticise it, expand it and extend it. I felt like an explorer about to set out across uncharted oceans, and the more I wrote the more excited I got at the prospect. The exams, accountancy and the stockbroker's office stood no chance. I decided to quit right away, before qualifying and going into my father's office. I knew that they were keeping a seat warm for me, but they would have no trouble in finding a replacement. My mother was away for a week and I decided to leave home then. I knew it was pointless trying to make her understand. She would say, as most people would, why not pass the exam first and then decide? But that was exactly what I didn't want to do. I didn't want to leave open the possibility of falling back on that qualification, in case I might be tempted to do so. So I left her a difficult letter and set off for London. I asked Jane to come down to collect me in the mini she had been lent by someone.

My mother was predictably furious. She had always disliked Jane. I had taken her home on occasions and she was not the sort she liked. Jane was not an English rose, she was a more exotic bloom, possibly poisonous, with her dark hair and black stockings. My mother was instinctively suspicious of her and blamed her for leading me astray. From that time on I was persona non grata at home. Overnight I became the black sheep. In fact Jane had nothing to do with the decision I made. It was entirely my own decision, based on an inner conviction that life had more to offer than an over-paid job in the City and the financial security that brought with it. There were deeper and higher things to be taken into account. I wanted to find out about them, to pursue my quest for the meaning of life, religion, God, the eternal mysteries that man has devoted so much thought to throughout history. Why should I be content to be an ant in that financial anthill, the City of London, a ghetto enclosing that self-important bunch of bank managers, when the mountains of knowledge, truth, beauty and love called me to a great adventure, to become an explorer, a pioneer perhaps? The discoveries I was in search of were in the realm of the intellect, the psyche. That was the great unknown world. It was into that vast darkness that I wanted to "let my little light shine". Not why me, but why not?

I had a choice, that was the point. I realised that I could drop into the mould that had been prepared for me, or I could take matters into my own hands and carve out my own destiny. I also realised that it was in making such choices that greatness lay. Now that may sound arrogant; what made me feel that I was so great? Nothing, but that didn't stop me wanting to make my own mark on the world. Arrogance was what provided the energy to make the decision, arrogance and sheer curiosity. I just wanted to know. What? Everything. I realised I knew nothing except how to think and I could use this one accomplishment to achieve my heart's desire. My heart and head were in unison. I was going to find out how it all worked, how it fitted together, what I really thought about things, not what I had been taught, but what I really thought myself when I took the time to look closely.

Soon after I had dropped out and embarked on the career of dharma bum I had a dream. It was so vivid that I have never forgotten it. I was standing in the entrance to a long changing room. It was actually the changing room of my prep school, quite typical, with a row of hooks along the wall on one side and narrow benches below them. On the opposite wall were basins and mirrors. The room was crowded and there was a tremendous scrum, everybody fighting to get a hook of their own. It occurred to me that there was no need to get hung up, so I threaded my way through the throng unnoticed to emerge from the door at the far end. I had a feeling of great peace.

On reflection, I can now make a more objective analysis of

my mother's attitude I think. She was upset of course that I was throwing up the chance to take my father's seat in his firm, a chance offered by his partners for her sake. She was annoyed that I hadn't given her the chance to dissuade me. She was angry that I had left the straight and narrow path which she had laid out for me, especially at the last moment. But, as I mentioned before, her love was conditional. As long as I was doing what she wanted, she loved me. The moment I took a decision on my own behalf her approval turned to disapproval. My behaviour was irresponsible, unforgivable. I now suspect that beneath this is a repressed guilt at her own behaviour much earlier, when she had "given me away" at ten months, which was now projected into me. In any case it didn't bother me. My mind was made up.

Now that I was free I took a new attitude to everything. Why not try pot? The next time Jane offered me a joint I smoked it. At first I got the giggles and just laughed at everything, then we listened to some Ray Charles. I haven't looked back since. I was amazed. To think this was what I had been afraid of. It made me laugh. The music was fantastic. It seemed to last for ever and I could hear each instrument quite clearly at the same time as all the others. Oh yes, now I knew what soul music was. Obviously Ray Charles was stoned out of his mind!

I had all my time to myself. I had no money, but Jane and her smoking friends were very helpful and I found that life still went on without money. The smoking world is much less concerned with the material things than the straight world. Smoking is in itself a very sociable ritual, with a circle of friends all getting high on the same joint. Everything is automatically shared. Soon I was a full-time smoker and as enthusiastic in praising the weed as I had previously been dismissive in refusing it. My concession to the need to make an income was to become a compulsive studier of the racing form and attempt to beat the bookies. Every morning I pored over the racing pages and worked out combinations of horses to put into accumulators, trebles and doubles in order to get some decent odds. My stakes were always minimal, rarely more than half a crown, now twelve and a half pennies in decimal coinage, except that we don't have half-pennies any more, or "haypnies" as they were pronounced – and after spending all afternoon in Manny King's betting shop in the Brompton Road, listening to all the commentaries from the racecourses up and down the country, sweating on the outcome, I would usually end up with roughly the same amount of money I had started with, though occasionally a big win would make it all worthwhile. I remember a two and six each way double making forty five pounds once and, even better, I once had a ten bob win treble which won me seventy pounds. I bought champagne to celebrate. My companion in the betting shop was Tony Bartlett, who had also been struggling with the accountancy course and who also gave it up in the end I think. At any rate he became very successful later in life in the building trade, with important Middle Eastern clients. Another punter who frequented that betting shop was Lucien Freud, who could be seen handing in his betting slips in the furtive way that seems characteristic of him.

Martin Wilkinson, one of Jane's friends, became a close friend. He was my modern jazz guru, introducing me to the sounds of Sonny Rollins, Coltrane, Miles Davis, Monk etc. We would get high to listen to the records, which I found essential for appreciating this difficult music. He also advised me to read Camus's book *The Rebel*, which made a deep impression. I liked the way Camus wrote and his explanation of the philosophy of the absurd in 'The Myth of Sisyphus' struck a chord and seemed exactly to describe man's predicament in a godless world. Yet there was something a bit pessimistic in it that didn't quite satisfy me. I felt there was a bit more to life than just accepting the absurdity of it, undeniable though that was.

It was early spring in 1963. Jane and her boyfriend, Michael Rainey, were going to drive to Torremolinos in southern Spain, where Michael's sister Shelagh lived. They offered to take me with them and I gladly accepted. Michael had an old Lancia. We hadn't gone a hundred kilometres in France when the car shuddered to a halt and subsided. It was a major problem and was going to take a long time to get the necessary parts and mend it. We went to Paris and stayed with Jimmy Douglas, an old friend of Michael's.

Paris was romantic and beautiful. We found some pills called Kinortine, which were available without prescription. There were forty in a bottle and four did the trick, though gradually we took more and more. Michael especially used to just swallow a whole bottle and take off at lightning speed. Jimmy was a rich American playboy, charming and handsome. For five years he had lived with Barbara Hutton, the Woolworths heiress, travelling round the world looking for the perfect doctor. His apartment in the Rue du Bac was large and comfortable. He had a grand piano and played classical music superbly. I was fascinated by the cafes in the Boulevard St Germain, the Deux Magots etc, and used to spend a lot of time sitting there, drinking pils and smoking endless cigarettes, taking to anyone I liked the look of. That was the beauty of speed, the ease with which one could make contact with strangers and the unflagging interest in everything that happened. In the evenings we would go with Jimmy and his friends to restaurants and night clubs, then perhaps Les Halles for breakfast. Every morning there was a huge jug of freshly made orange juice. The car remained unmended for two months. When it was finally done, Jane and Michael decided to return to London before going on. I stayed in Paris for a week or two and then went back too.

In London the sun was shining. I had brought some Kinortine with me from Paris and there was plenty of pot around. I was writing a lot during this period. In Paris I had sat up all one night and written solidly for sixteen hours. I hardly knew what I was writing, but it amounted to over 20,000 words, nearly all of it in rhyming couplets, on the theme of love, heaven and hell. The hell bit came at the end when I was really coming down from the last fifteen Kinortine. The words just streamed out of me, through me and through my pen onto the paper. It was automatic writing. I was a mere vehicle for this stream of consciousness that flowed like a river out of my mind.

I revelled in the freedom of having all my time for myself. I roamed London with Jishy, a brilliant teenage cousin of Jane's, discussing all the problems from god to the creation of the universe, from politics to the injustices of society. Jishy's grandfather was prime minister at the time and his father was an MP and he therefore felt these things very keenly. We used to walk vast distances, talking all the time, oblivious to where we were, from Notting Hill Gate to Chelsea across Hyde Park, dropping in to his parents' house in Victoria to raid the fridge, always well-stocked with delicious remains from political dinner parties, to assuage the pangs of hunger. I got stoned all the time and went to parties and discotheques to pick up girls. I didn't find a permanent girlfriend, but I was weaning myself from all the old ideas and I had enjoyable nights with different girls.

At one party I met Suna. She was tall, blonde and beautiful, and I was strongly attracted to her. I asked her to come with me and have breakfast with some other people after the party had ended. It was still dark. Martin, Jane, Michael and several others were there. When we had had breakfast dawn was not far away. Suna said she lived just near there and had some pot. Why didn't we go and smoke some? Everyone was too tired except me and Martin. We went with Suna and had a smoke. She was going to San Francisco shortly. She told me she had been living in Torremolinos with an American for three years, but now they had split up. She wanted a change and time to think things over and was going to San Francisco for a few weeks to get right away from Europe. I saw quite a lot of her in the following days. We talked a lot and went for long walks. I told her I was going to Torremolinos and she said she might join me there after coming back. I didn't make a pass at her, not being sure that she wanted me to. I thought well if she comes to Torremolinos then I will know for sure. She gave me some names and addresses in Torremolinos and I drove her to the airport in a borrowed car. Martin turned up and came too.

Michael and Jane had already left for Spain, but Michael had given me a ticket, so now I flew out and joined them. There I met Shelagh, Michael's sister. She was attractive and fun and I liked her. She was having an affair with a nightclub owner who had been one of the leaders of the OAS in Algeria. He toted a gun and was quite charming, but a bit sinister, a gangster in fact. Michael and Jane did not think much of Torremolinos and they soon left, but I stayed on. I looked up some of the people Suna had recommended and particularly liked Claire, a Jewish American writer. She was very intelligent, dark and attractive. Our passion bloomed and then subsided into friendship. Claire was divorced and lived with her three children in a nice house on the beach. I stayed with her for quite some time and became very fond of her.

Jaime, a friend of Michael and Shelagh's, who lived down the coast in Marbella, got me a job teaching the two sons of a marquesa to speak English. They were aged three and five and could hardly speak Spanish, let alone English. As I could speak no Spanish, it was a good opportunity to study the basics. I only taught them for three hours a week for 1,000 pesetas (£6) and that was enough for food, cigarettes and grass. Spain was very cheap in those days and one could live quite well on 50 pesetas a day. Torremolinos was full of weird individuals from all over the place, the majority Americans; beatniks, musicians, painters, poets and pushers. Everybody smoked pot, at least everybody on the scene I moved in. For me it was a great university of life and I thoroughly enjoyed myself. There were lovely girls looking for romance and a refreshing lack of convention. All the foreigners there had come to escape the restrictions of their native societies, and indeed so had a few Spaniards by merging with the aliens.

The centre of the weirdo scene was Pedro's bar in the plaza in the middle of town. Pedro was an ex Madison Avenue executive who had left America for a life of hedonism in the sun. He ran the bar with a flourish, wearing fancy clothes and encouraging all kinds of eccentricity. His partner in ownership was Tim Willoughby, an English peer from London, equally flamboyant but richer. He also owned the Lali Lali nightclub where there was a resident jazz group composed of four European musicians. Jacques Sterne was one of the stars in the Pedro's galaxy. He had got polio when he was seventeen and lost the use of his legs. However that didn't stop him having a good time. He had a beautiful girlfriend who lived with him and he drank everyone under the table as well as smoking pot all day with cigarettes to fill the gaps. He also took twice the lethal dose of sleeping pills every night, and speed too. He was very proud of having kicked the junk habit. He had been living with Bill Burroughs while he was writing *Naked Lunch* and they had kicked the habit together. He warned me never to take heroin and I took his advice. He became my atheist guru. In all night sessions with him and others I was finally convinced that God was a fiction. Man invented him, not vice versa. Later I understood that, in Freudian terms, he was the projection of the father in the infantile mind of the adult. With regards to the evolution of language and thought, primitive man was of course an infant.

Suna wrote to me from San Francisco saying that she was coming later. Later she rang from London. Later still she wrote from Tunis, saying she had been invited by Martin to stay there with a friend of his and would be coming on from there. This surprised me. Finally, when they both arrived, Suna told me that she had fallen in love with Martin and was going to live with him. They got a house up in the mountains, some twenty kilometres from Torremolinos. I saw them periodically and remained friends with them.

As the summer wore on and the heat increased events got madder and madder. There were fights in the Lali Lali. Tim Willoughby and Jacques were rival gurus and they vied with each other to be the centre of the scene. Both were rich and surrounded with beatniks and chicks. They lived in neighbouring houses and all night their feud could be heard in the street as they slanged each other from their respective patios, insulting each other's race and intellect. Shelagh decided to marry one of her mother's ex-lovers, a-sixty-year-old man who lived in a beautiful villa high up in the mountains. She was given a car and an apartment in town, where she carried on her affair with the gangster, who was also married. Her husband was an erudite man who stayed in his villa and wrote passionate poems to his young wife while she sported around on the coast below. However she had to spend some time with her husband and, as she couldn't stand living with him alone, she invited me to stay up there. For a time I lived in a shed in the garden on a camp bed. It was beautiful. At night the walls were covered with geckos. In the daytime I swam in the pool which was filled with running water from mountain streams and was icy cold. Shelagh drove down to Torremolinos frequently, so I kept in touch and kept myself supplied with pot and pills for my long sessions of writing in the hills. I also had long conversations with David, Shelagh's husband. He had a great love and knowledge of Milton. I think he was glad of my company.

Finally I moved down to town again when Tim offered me a room in his house while he went to the south of France. It was a fatal journey. He went with his best friend, another wealthy, speed-loving young man, and they set out from the Cote d'Azur in a speedboat during a force thirteen gale. Neither of them was ever seen again. Rumours abounded in Torremolinos that the police had been after Tim and he had staged the whole thing to disappear and was now in the Polynesian islands founding a master race, but confirmation never reached my ears. Jacques offered me a room in his house and I moved next door. Jacques's girlfriend was half French and half Russian, called Selene. She had at one time been an haute couture model in Paris, but then had dropped out and become an opium addict. After six years she had kicked opium and was now making do with alcohol, pot and sleepers. She was a fiery person, with piercing eyes and hollow cheeks, always on the verge of suicide, while Jacques was afraid that she might kill him in a fit of jealousy.

In the autumn I decided to return to London for the winter. The night before I left I had supper with Selene in a snack bar in town and she poured out her heart to me, telling me how miserable she was. I did what I could to cheer her up and then we went to Pedro's for a drink. At the bar Jacques was sitting talking to another girl. Selene flew into a rage, picked up one of Jacques's crutches and started hitting him over the head with it. There was a tremendous commotion. It took three hefty waiters to hold Selene down. Some little creep called the police in and she was taken off to spend the night in a cell. I left the next day but later heard that she had committed suicide three days after that.

London was depressing and cold. I got a temporary job in an accountant's office and lived in a dreary bed-sitter in Chelsea. During the winter I made my first attempt to write a novel. I wrote it, but it fell between the two stools of novel and autobiography. It had a good title: *Way In – Way Out*. Jane and Michael were in London, but they had made other friends and I did not see as much of them as before. Jishy was now at Oxford and getting hooked on junk. Over Christmas his parents sent him to a clinic in Switzerland to be withdrawn. He came back very depressed. In the spring Martin wrote from Spain to say that David had bought Shelagh a bar in T-town and she was desperate for someone to run the financial side of things. At once I wrote to her applying for the job and she accepted the application.

The bar was called Shelagh's Bar. It was a jolly place, with six attractive young Spanish barmen who ensured a constant nucleus of homosexual patrons in their middle age. The waiters' *piéce de résistance* was a sort of dance routine, which involved mixing cocktails while flinging the bottles, ice-filled shaker and glasses from one to another in time to the music. They would do this periodically for the duration of a record – the Searchers' 'Needles and Pins' was a favourite – at the same time stirring the emotions of their admirers to boiling point. Around this nucleus revolved a whirling mass of teenage tourists attracted by the latest pop records of the Beatles and Stones, which blared out all night over the clinking Cuba Libres. A succession of hustler managers had reduced it to the verge of bankruptcy, but business was good and balance was soon restored, though it did involve explaining to the owner that she couldn't just pocket all the takings when the bar closed and go out spending.

Shelagh was still carrying on with the gangster, whose bar was next door, though the relationship seemed a bit frayed. For a while I hitched up with an attractive American girl called Sue, who had an enchanting three-year-old daughter (by a New York cop) called Tracy. I rented a room on top of the flat roof of a villa. It stood on stilts, like a little pagoda, with a pointed roof of shiny tiles. The flat roof of the villa made a terrace all around it. A flight of four wooden steps led up to the door and there were windows on three sides looking out over the sea and the distant mountains. The tops of palm trees in the garden below were at eye level and shoots of jasmine climbed up the side of the house and onto the terrace. I could pick sprigs of it to keep the mosquitoes off. There was an outside shower I could use at the bottom of the steps which led up to the roof, so I was completely self-contained. It was a beautiful place and I felt like a king in his castle up there. In the daytime I sat on the roof and smoked pot while writing poetry and then in the evening, from eight to two, I hovered in the background at the bar.

One night, after a month or two, Shelagh asked me to help her back to her villa with some records. The villa had replaced the apartment and had a garden. We had a drink and listened to some records and ended up making love all night. The sex was marvellous and we didn't look back. I kept my room on the roof, but spent more and more time with Shelagh.

One day Jishy appeared out of the blue. He stayed for a week or so in my room, smoking all day with Murray, a Canadian beatnik friend of mine, who liked to spend a lot of time on the roof. Murray was so quiet that he could pass through customs from Morocco with a backpack full of kif without anyone noticing he was there. I was more interested in Shelagh at this time and was absent a lot. I think Jishy was disappointed that I hadn't more time to spend with him and one day he announced he was leaving, as suddenly as he had arrived. He went back to England for the next term at Oxford. His doctor gave him some tranquillisers. On the first night of the term he went to a party and got drunk, taking a bottle of whisky back to his room. The combination of the tranquillisers and alcohol was lethal and he died that night. He was nineteen.

That summer was fun. There was never a dull moment. I spent more and more time with Shelagh. Our relationship was based on sexual compatibility and was not destroyed by the random excursions of either of us. We didn't agree on many things, but that didn't matter to me. Shelagh was just fun to be with. Things were always happening, often unexpected, as she tumbled from one happening into the next. She had a great way with people, who couldn't resist her infectious personality and she had a straightforward openness which was very attractive. That was the bright side, but there was a dark side too, an inner insecurity which belied the outer confidence. She was always taking overdoses of sleeping tablets and once she drank a whole bottle of vodka at one swipe and passed out into a coma, her face all puffed up. After every overdose the doctor insisted that suicide was illegal in Spain. Shelagh was an alcoholic pillhead, who disapproved of pot. "You must give up drugs Joey" she used to say. When she asked me one night if we might have a baby, I agreed. I loved her and I was happy. It seemed quite natural in that setting. The fact that she was married had long since ceased to have any meaning, as she never saw David. They were separated.

In the autumn Shelagh decided to sell the bar and move to Italy. I didn't want to go at first, since I was having a good time in Spain, but in the end I agreed to go. I wanted to have another go at writing a book and perhaps in the hills above Florence would be a good place to do so. The book was to be built around the experience I had had one glorious night that summer when Allan had turned me on to mescalinee.

Allan Cisco was not his real name, just the one he used. He was a spade hustler from Boston. He had been turned on by the Leary crowd in Mexico when they were doing research into the effects of psychedelic drugs on a group of people over a two month period. Allan told me how he had gone swimming on mescaline at midnight down in Acapulco and hallucinated wrestling with a giant octopus in the waves. His favourite phrase was "mind at large". He said his game was to move in on the hip crowd wherever he went and become "resident spade". "Mind at large" he used to say to all and sundry and leave everyone wondering what he meant. He had the coolest image in town, padding about with eyes concealed behind the essential shades. I have always been impressed by the American "cool" and I was attracted by Allan's image. He seemed to like me too, for he had only two trips left and he gave me one of them.

At last I had found what I was looking for, heaven on earth. I had wild hallucinations, at one moment feeling that the bed I was lying on was a tropical sea and I was part of it as blissful waves swept through and over me, then seeing the walls, ceiling and floor and the air in the room seething with insects of every kind, shape and size. My instant recoil was quickly forgotten as I gazed at the beauty of them and each one burnt with the most vivid colours I'd ever seen and seemed like unearthly jewels. Only when I went to pick one up my fingers passed through it without feeling anything, because it wasn't really there. Later I saw a real one and exclaimed in delight, "Look, a real insect!". The peach I held in my hand was too beautiful to describe. It was the universe I was holding. I bit into it. It tasted like ambrosia and where my teeth had bitten fresh colours darted and flowed in the juice. I had taken the mescaline in a studio on the roof of Claire's house, with a terrace around it. Standing on the terrace I could see a cliff about a quarter of a mile away, on top of which was a building site. I saw a space ship land on the clifftop and I could see a restaurant in the space ship with waiters moving around between the tables. Then, as my eyes moved down the cliff below I saw a group of

Red Indians on their ponies being pursued by the US Cavalry, just like in a movie but apparently for real. There they were in front of my eyes, galloping frantically down through the trees with clouds of dust rising from their hooves. It was incredible, fantastic, ecstatic. I could see for miles, impersonate anybody, do anything with the greatest of ease. I laughed and laughed at the sheer joy of existence and seemed to share the joke with the stars. I mean what does keep the heart beating on? For four or five hours I was up on the highest level and then gradually began coming down. Finally, some twelve hours after taking the trip, it was over and I fell asleep.

Now that I had been up there I knew that there was where I wanted to stay. At the height of the trip I had looked in the mirror and seen the faces of all the members of my family look back at me in turn where my face should have been. Having assumed for some time that I must have some problem (I mean everyone has some problem, don't they?), I asked myself what it was. The answer was that I had no problem on mescaline. I had felt that whatever needed doing I could do quite easily. The only problem was to get more mescaline. At that time, 1964, there were not many psychedelic drugs around. I was told that LSD was as good as mescaline, but I couldn't find any of that either. It became my main ambition to regain that miraculous state of mind. I had been to the top of the mountain and the view from there was so comprehensive and magnificent that nothing less high would satisfy me. Meanwhile life went on and soon Shelagh and I set off for Italy, with Shelagh's five-year-old daughter Camilla, from an earlier love affair.

On a Tuscan hillside covered with olive groves and cypress trees we found a little house to rent. I took a room in the local pension to write in and spent most of the daytime there. It was very peaceful. We saw no one else and, since we hadn't got a lot to talk about to each other, Shelagh got fairly bored. I read a lot and wrote my book, called "I Think". It centred on the mescaline trip, with a "know yourself and know god" message, but it still wasn't good enough. I was glad I'd done it, for the practise; my head was full of ideas, but I found they were not cohesive enough to fill a book with. I knew that turning on was the way to self-knowledge, but I didn't know why or how it worked. To be high was the cure for the dullness and seriousness of "straight" life, with its roles that you were supposed to fit into, but what exactly it was, what was actually happening in the mind – these were the questions that I couldn't answer. It wasn't enough just to say you've got to get high. How exactly did being high bring the beatific vision, the kernel of the beatnik movement? What exactly was the mystical experience? I knew I was on the track of the essence of religion, that the pursuit of self-knowledge was not just a lotus-eater's dream but rather a vital part of achieving true happiness and peace of mind. These things were important. It was so easy to be lured down the straight and narrow path of getting a good job and settling in the mud, but the price you paid was to sacrifice the spirit of youth. Was that just an excuse? Was I basically just lazy? Yes, but no. I wanted to find my own path, not follow one laid out for me. I wanted to think it all through and come to my own conclusions. I wanted to find the truth, but what did I mean by that? What truth? The truth about the origin of religions perhaps, the truth about myself. There were so many problems and questions I wanted to grapple with. I had to think and think about it all and, above all, I needed time.

Every now and then we went down to Florence and it was in a clinic there that Shelagh's pregnancy test proved positive. We celebrated with champagne. The other memorable event during the two to three months we were there was a thunderstorm. Hailstones as large as golf balls rained out of the sky with such force as I had never dreamed of. Fortunately I was indoors in the pension. The first sign of something unusual was the cracking of the windowpane. I closed the shutters just before the real thing burst. The noise was deafening. I wondered what would happen to anyone caught out in it. I felt very puny in the face of such elemental power. When it was over I went across the road to Shelagh and Camilla. Three windows in our house had been shattered, but they were alright.

Shelagh was on a course of tranquillisers while we were in Italy and she hardly drank at all. This made her much quieter than usual and her health improved. However there was not much to do and when I had finished my book I too was at a loose end. Shelagh had to go to London anyhow, to collect the balance of the money from the sale of the bar, so that was our next stop.

For a month or two things went alright in London, but then they began to deteriorate. We had planned to spend Christmas with Michael and Jane at her parents' empty country estate. Just before we were due to go we had two separate but simultaneous domestic rows. Michael and Shelagh supported each other and decided not to go, so Jane and I went ahead, expecting them to follow later. They did not come however and when I returned to London Shelagh had moved house and no one would tell me where she had gone. In view of the approaching birth of our child I was beginning to feel that I should get a job and think about supporting my family. I regretted very much having to give up my freedom so soon, but I was prepared to do so.

One day I was told that Shelagh was in St George's Hospital and the baby had been born prematurely. I rushed to the maternity ward and had my first sight of our daughter, Titania, lying in an incubator. She had jaundice and was a beautiful golden brown colour. She didn't look like a baby, rather an exceedingly miniature adult; she wasn't pink and chubby, but slim and brown. Shelagh was alright and I proposed to her that I get a job and look for a house in London. She said she wasn't sure she wanted to live in London and wanted time to think about it. Meanwhile I started to look for a job in publishing or a newspaper. Before I had got anything fixed up Shelagh said she didn't want to live with me in London. I tried to persuade her to change her mind, since my best job prospects were there, but she was adamant. That altered my plans. There was no point getting a job and settling down without Shelagh and Titania. I decided to leave England again and continue following my invisible star. I took the train to Torremolinos, hoping to find something to do out there.

In T-town Jacques was there with a beautiful new wife, a young and very intelligent Spanish girl called Dolores. He offered me a room in his house. There were a lot of old faces around: Jimmy, from Paris, was there with Brian Epstein, the Beatles' manager, and Lionel Bart, the songwriter. I was fairly depressed, but Argus, a lovely black girl from New York, whom I had known from before, soon comforted me and cheered me up. One night as I was with Argus in a nightclub Shelagh walked in. She hadn't brought the baby, but had come to see if I wanted to give it a try out here. I agreed to try and get a job and an apartment and Shelagh went back to London till I had got things arranged.

One night, as I was sitting in Pedro's, I saw a stunningly beautiful girl sit down at the same table. She was tall, dark and Polynesian looking. Her name was Dori and she was part French, part Philippino and part American. She was on holiday from New York with her daughter, having left her film director husband behind. She was attracted to me too and we had a passionate affair for two weeks. I remember walking along the beach at dawn, singing "There will never be another you" to her. I tried to persuade her to stay on and she seemed ready to. She used to leave her daughter, who was nine, asleep in her apartment and spend the night with me in Jacques's house, then return early in the morning before her daughter woke up. We would both get some sleep and then meet again for lunch. One morning when I got round to her apartment and knocked, there was no answer. Then I saw a note in the empty milk bottle outside the door. On it was written "Joey" about a hundred times and nothing else. She had flown. Later I got a letter from her, written on the flight back to New York.

I went down the coast and stayed with Jaime in Marbella. He knew of a restaurant out in the country in need of a manager. The owner always went to England in the summer, and he was sure it was the perfect job for me and Shelagh, me to run the place and Shelagh to look pretty and provide personality. Shelagh came out with Titania and Camilla and we arranged to go out and talk it over with the owner, who wanted to see us both. However things didn't work out so smoothly. Shelagh started drinking again and going out on the town and after a week we still hadn't got to see the owner. I was very frustrated. I could see that Shelagh wanted me to make a bigger sacrifice than I was prepared to make, so I made up my mind to leave her. It was a completely selfish decision, in the interests of self-preservation.

I went back to Torremolinos, very depressed. My life was at its lowest ebb. For all my high-flown ideas about freedom, what had I come to? I had brought an innocent child into the world and was now running away from my responsibility to her. My freedom had brought me nothing. I had no money, I hadn't written anything worth publishing, all I had was a spark of hope still. I felt that my destiny beckoned me on and something would happen to make it all worthwhile. Martin wrote from Majorca. I knew that Luciano, a friend from Torremolinos, was in Ibiza and I thought perhaps that was the place to go. Jacques gave me the fare for Majorca and Martin bought me a ticket for Ibiza. There I found Luciano with a spare bed in his house.

It was the summer of '65. Ibiza was a beatnik's paradise, sunny and beautiful, the centre of the Mediterranean smoking world. At one time it seemed like a Noah's Ark for smokers. Every nationality was represented. It had recently become a popular location for making films and the smokers could earn 300 pesetas a day as extras, which involved sitting in the sun, waiting and smoking. Since this is what many of them would have been doing anyway, it was a good job. One could live well for a week on 300 pesetas. The difference between Ibiza and Torremolinos, which by now had become a poor man's Miami, was that in Torremolinos there were five hundred tourists for every smoker while in Ibiza there were almost as many smokers as tourists. Sue and Tracy were there. I was glad to see them. Sue had taken LSD once and she told me that she was expecting some to arrive in the near future.

Throughout the smoking community acid was the big new subject. Very few had taken it at that time, but everybody was waiting for it. Jacques sent me some money from T-town to get some for him when it came. Sue was working at a millionaires' country club some twenty kilometres from the city. She had a small car. The millionaire owner, a Belgian who had been forced to leave his mines in the Congo after independence, wanted someone to sort out the accounts of his mining concerns, but could find no one in Ibiza to do it. Sue knew that I had that training and asked me if I wanted the job. For two weeks or so I went every day with her to the country club and produced the analyses and schedules required. That earned me 11,000 pesetas (£66), which set me up for the summer. I can well remember the pleasant drives with Sue and Tracy through the countryside. At a particular place along the road there was a patch of open ground where they laid the apricots out to dry. There was an acre or more of them and the pungent smell was wafted on the heat through the open windows of the car. Things were looking up. I had somewhere to live and enough money, supplemented by occasional days as an extra, to cover the foreseeable future. As the weeks went by the acid still did not arrive, but there was plenty to smoke and it was a nice place to wait for Godot.

One day Luciano and I went to visit Donna, a friend of his who lived in Figueretas, a suburb separated from the old city by the hollow hill which contains a labyrinth of Phoenician tombs. Access to the tombs was only by one hole in the mountain, where the caretaker sat in front of the gate. I went down once and remember the total darkness when the caretaker switched off the electric light, pitch black darkness. With the light on I could see a few skeletons in open tombs, carved like chests out of the rock, and a maze of passages that extended far beyond the light's penetration. It was an eerie experience.

Anyway, we were visiting Donna, and while we were there Donna's neighbour, an attractive American girl called Fran, came in with two men. Fran chatted to Donna for a minute or two while the two men carried on with their conversation. The only remark I remember was one saying to the other: "so now do you see a future in LSD?" When they had gone Donna told us that one of them, the one whose remark I had noticed, was Bart Huges, the Dutchman who had drilled a hole in his skull to get permanently high. I had heard of this earlier in Torremolinos, but had put it down as a crankish idea and had discounted the likelihood anyhow. So that was he, and he had really done it. He looked normal enough, but I had been more interested in the appearance of Fran.

Later I went round there again and called on Fran. She told me that Bart had gone to Amsterdam to get some acid and would be back in a week or two. She was trying to find buyers for it. I told her that I had some money for that purpose and wanted to buy as much as possible, to send some to Jacques and take some myself. I accompanied Fran into town to look for other customers and asked her all about the hole in the head. She told me it was done to increase the volume of blood in the brain. I was sceptical of this, because I thought you can't change the balance of nature. If you gained more blood you must lose something else and the gain would be cancelled out by the loss. Fran didn't know all the details, so I couldn't reach a final judgement on the matter.

Anyway, more to the point, at last I had found the acid. Now it was a matter of waiting for Bart.

I saw Fran quite often. Besides being very attractive, she was intelligent and friendly. One day I walked her home from Ibiza, hoping to get to know her better. At the door of her apartment she slipped in and whispered that she wasn't feeling sociable that evening. A few days later I called on her again. She said she had read her stars and they said she should expect an important visitor soon, so she was expecting Bart in the next day or two. Since it was about two weeks since my first call, this seemed entirely reasonable. She told me what time the boat arrived and the next morning I was waiting at the Alhambra café. Someone pointed out Bart among a group of arriving travellers. I went up to him, introduced myself and asked whether he had got the acid. He had. He told me to come to Figueretas that evening to get it.

I arrived not a minute late. Bart told me that Fran and he were going to take a trip that night and asked if I would like to take my first trip with them. I gladly accepted the offer. We agreed to take it in Luciano's house in the old town. It was to be Fran's first trip too. Bart told us that it was necessary to take extra sugar with the trip and said that he would get it.

We met at a prearranged time and place. Bart was carrying a large brown paper bag full of sugarlumps and lemons. In the house we squeezed the juice from the lemons into saucers. Then we took the trips. Bart advised us to start taking sugar right away and set the example by dipping sugarlumps into the lemon juice and eating them. We both did likewise. After about an hour we were on top of the world. I was expecting hallucinations and when I went into the bathroom and found that a pipe had burst and water was leaking all over the floor, I couldn't make my mind up if it was real or imagined. It seemed real, it even felt wet, but I knew from experience that it still might not be. In fact it was and the next day my bed was three inches deep in water. Luckily the bed had legs. At the time it was fascinating, but it never occurred to me to do anything about it. I knew I was as high as I had been on mescaline, and I was finding out that you could be that high without hallucinating. I kept eating the sugarlumps and I felt very happy. I had boundless energy and as I began to get used to life at that height I felt the tremendous potential it brought. Up here, if you could separate the real from the illusory, you could do anything you wanted. It was the most positive experience. I felt brilliant, god-like, able to understand everything. At the same time as being fascinated by the way I could see things as if through a magnifying glass, I could also hear all the sounds of the town outside the house as well as those inside and each perception registered quite clearly, distinct from all the others though related to them, like the various instruments in an orchestra. Now I knew what eternity meant. Time seemed to stop and still everything was moving. Nothing was too small to be considered. Everything had its place in the scheme of things and was equally interesting: the form, the structure, the colour, the connection, the eternal cycle of life. This was where it was at. I was ecstatic. I kept eating sugarlumps. I could feel that this was the energy I needed to get around this universe in my brain.

After we had been high for maybe two hours, the window opened and in through it jumped Allan. By now I knew that my reality-testing apparatus was working properly, so I figured that this was no hallucination. Still it was a surprise. He had just arrived from Torremolinos. I gave him a trip and he swallowed it at once. Luciano came up and I gave him one too. Bart and Fran decided to go home. Before leaving, Bart gave me a stencilled description of the mechanism of brainbloodvolume, as he called it, and then invited Allan and me over the next night for another trip. I went on eating sugar, even though Allan had never heard anything about that and was sceptical about it. The trip lasted all night long. Several other people came round and we sat up talking until the dawn. As the sun came up the trip came to an end and the magic wore off. I went to sleep in my waterlogged bed.

When I woke up I felt very good, without hangover. I read Bart's description of the various ways to expand consciousness by increasing the volume of blood in the brain capillaries. The brain needs blood to function. It is from the blood that the braincells take their oxygen and glucose, which they combust to do their work. The way the circulation works is this: the blood flows from the heart through the arteries into the capillaries, tiny elastic (literally hair-like) vessels from which the cells take their nutrients and into which they discharge the waste product of their metabolism, carbon dioxide. The blood is then carried back through the veins to the lungs, where the carbon dioxide is exhaled and fresh oxygen inhaled, as the blood returns to the heart for another go round. With more blood in the brain capillaries more brain cells can function simultaneously, which means total consciousness is expanded. Drugs (including LSD) work by constricting the veins, thus causing the capillaries to expand with a resulting increase in their volume. With extra blood in the brain there is a greater consumption of glucose, which I later learnt is the sole source of energy for the brain. I saw that there was a loss of cerebrospinal fluid corresponding to the increase of brainbloodvolume.

As I had no idea what cerebrospinal fluid was, I was still unable to judge whether the loss of it was a disadvantage, but I was quite sure that there was an advantage in increasing the brainbloodvolume (a word I at first considered hideous and indigestible, but eventually came to like, because it simplified the concept of the total volume of blood in the brain capillaries). I decided to ask Bart more about the whole thing. I had never before thought about consciousness in such a purely materialistic way. Of course I knew that blood flowed through every organ in the body, but the idea of increasing the volume of blood to improve the function had never crossed my mind. There are of course other examples of this, perhaps the most obvious being an erection, and in fact the correlation between function and blood volume in organs is the rule. The blood goes where the action is. For some years I had been puzzling over what happened in the brain when one got high without ever finding out, and now I was presented with a picture that made complete sense.

This first trip on LSD, with sugar, changed my life. Apart from the extraordinary perception experienced, there was one very obvious way in which it did this. I had been a nicotine addict for eight years. My habit at that time was sixty cigarettes a day. I had one going more or less all the time. Once before, at Oxford, I had given up smoking for eight weeks while I was in training for boxing. Then I had noticed the great difference it made to my breathing. On ten mile runs I had found my breathing was deeper and easier. Then my addiction had been in its infancy, so giving up had not been too hard to do. Now, on acid, for the first four or five hours the thought of having a cigarette didn't occur to me, but in the second half, coming down, my habit reasserted itself and I started lighting one after another. The next day I found three-quarters-unsmoked cigarettes all over the house. That night, on my next trip, the same thing happened. As I took a deep drag on the first one I lit, I had the reaction I'd had as a child on smoking my first cigarette behind a haystack. I felt sick, my knees went weak and I thought ugh, how disgusting this is. I realised that I really didn't like these things. Of course my instinctive reaction had been right. At the time it had been more important to be like Humphrey Bogart or James Dean, but now I realised that I was being poisoned and I didn't like it. I gave up smoking there and then, with no trouble at all.

It was obvious to anyone who met Bart that he was someone who knew what he was talking about. He came from a family of doctors and had a thorough knowledge of medical science. He never blustered or tried to blind one with scientific jargon. Ask him a question and he answered it in the simplest way he could. What more could one want from a teacher?

That night, when Allan and I went round and took another trip, I asked Bart what cerebrospinal fluid (csf) was. He told me that it consists mainly of water and that the whole central nervous system "floats" in it. There is no space within the central nervous system. Wherever there would be space within it there was csf. He explained that the loss of some of it, which had been my main reservation about the mechanism, had no disadvantageous results. There was too much of it in the brain of the adult; the problem was how to get rid of the superfluous volume, and the only way to do that permanently was by trepanation.

Gradually the picture became clear to me. Man's upright position, with neck vertical, meant that the volume of blood in the brain was held up in defiance of gravity. When man stood upright the ratio of blood to csf in the brain altered; the brain lost blood and gained csf. Blood is heavier than csf and is therefore more vulnerable to gravity in the upright position, especially since csf circulates only in the central nervous system (brain and spinal column), thus having "squatter's rights", so to speak. Unlike the blood, it has nowhere else to go; to get rid of any requires pressure. The venous constriction caused by drugs creates a resistance which causes the pulsepressure to build up in the capillaries and exert itself on the volume of csf in the brain, some of which is then squeezed out of the central nervous system through the nerve channels. This is what we call getting high. By squeezing out csf we make room for more blood and thus expand our consciousness.

No other animals defied the laws of nature like this, and no other animals suffered like man, with his neuroses and psychoses and general physical debility, not to mention his wars and persecutions. Any animal that survives can perform his natural functions without difficulty; not so man. The bird can reach the root of every feather on its body, the monkey leaps from tree to tree; compare that with the attempts of many people over twenty five to touch their toes. Man has indeed fallen from the animal state. So great is his misunderstanding that only in the present century has a small minority come to accept that he is an animal, while the rest still think he is something superior. Could it really be that this is due to his assumption of the upright position? There must have been advantages in it for man to have survived. They are plain to see: the freeing of the hands for making and using tools and weapons, the ability to see further and run faster, probably indirectly the development of speech. Could it be that there was also a disadvantage? Yes, that is so, and that was Bart's teaching.

At the end of growth (generally between the ages of eighteen and twenty-one) the sutures in the skull (seams between the separate plates of bone) seal together, encasing the brain in one rigid structure of bone. Before that the heartbeat can express itself in the brain arteries, as can be seen and felt in the baby's open fontanels. For this pulsation to exist there must be some give in the surrounding tissue. Once the skull has sealed there is no longer any give in the substance surrounding the brain membranes. The pulsation is suppressed. The intra-cranial pressure which this pulsation exerts is lost. It had been keeping the capillaries blown up. Now they shrink. Gravity claims a certain amount of blood, which is automatically replaced by the lighter csf, produced inside the central nervous system.

This reduction of the brainbloodvolume means that the brain as a whole loses some of its potential function, since the braincells depend on the supply of blood to perform their individual functions. The spontaneity and creativity of childhood diminish. From now on rationing must be introduced in order to keep optimal function in the parts most essential to survival, in particular the speech centres. Here begins the problem unique to man, the need for repression, the problem at the root of all his other mental problems, as Freud pointed out. With a limited volume of blood, to keep the speech centres functioning, function in other parts of the brain has to be repressed. This is the essence of Bart's discovery: paradise lost (the Fall of Mankind) is the blood (consciousness) lost in the brain as a result of standing upright, compounded by the further loss that follows the sealing of the skull at the end of growth. It is this last loss that is restored by trepanation. The lost pulsepressure is restored. Imagine the brain membranes as the membrane of a drum, reverberating with each beat of the heart. The sealing of the skull prevents this reverberation taking place.

Once I had grasped the main points of Bart's teaching, I realised that this was an extremely important discovery, casting light as it does on the most vital yet mysterious part of life, the working of the brain. I was elated to have stumbled into it so near the beginning, so that I could play a part in spreading the news to an unknowing world. This was the knowledge I had been lacking in my attempts to persuade everyone of the value of getting high. The breadth of awareness and the sense of eternity, attributes of the divine which together provided this feeling of universal unity, were both a consequence of the increased brain metabolism that came from more cells functioning simultaneously. Whilst trepanation restored the youthful level of brain metabolism to the brain, LSD did a lot more. The high achieved was the maximum possible; Olympian you could call it.

There are different levels of consciousness, depending on the total number of brain cells functioning at the same time, which depends on the volume of blood available, ie the total volume of blood in the brain capillaries (brainbloodvolume). The constriction of veins caused by LSD is strong and long-lasting, enough to flood the brain with blood as it were. I should explain at this point that the arteries have nerves attached to them, so that the blood flow is regulated by the central nervous system, which can thus counter the effect of a vaso-constricting substance in the blood to keep the flow constant. The veins, however, do not have nerves attached to them, so the same substance will cause them to constrict, with the inevitable effect that the capillaries will expand. The effect of taking LSD therefore is that the whole brain comes alight, and it is indeed light in a very literal sense. To me there is something supremely beautiful in the cycle whereby sunlight is encapsulated in sugar, via photosynthesis, and then reappears in the form of consciousness when the glucose is oxidised in the brain. The more brain cells that are functioning simultaneously the brighter the light. I, for one, could never be happy with a forty watt bulb in my head once I had got used to a hundred.

In my relationship with Bart I fell naturally into the role of younger brother. I asked him a host of questions I had always wanted to know the answer to and in most cases he knew the answer. If he didn't, he said so.

Allan couldn't follow the thinking all the way through. Consequently he rejected it and put it down as Bart's power game. I tried to persuade him to test the effectiveness of sugar-taking to counter what Bart called the "sugarlack" that resulted from increasing the blood volume. I explained that, with more blood to feed from, the brain used up more glucose than usual, which meant the bloodsugar level fell, with the accompanying symptoms of perceptual distortions, hallucinations, paranoia etc, all well know to medical science or any diabetic for that matter. Taking sugar on acid enabled one to think clearly on the highest level and keep one's attention focused on what one wanted. Allan thought I had been taken in by a rival guru and was too suspicious to try it even once.

Bart was at that time looking for someone to help him with the description of the mechanism in English. I was only too happy to be the one. For the next few months I worked with him and Fran on the wording of the scroll "Homo Sapiens Correctus", in which he described eight different methods of increasing the brainbloodvolume with diagrams. By the end I realised that the whole story was told in the diagrams, but I would never have understood it so well without having to think how I would put in simple English what Bart explained to me. This was a task fit for any writer. Bart's English was good but not perfect. It usually meant shortening his sentences to leave the bare bones of the sense. It was an unforgettable and immensely rewarding experience. I learnt more in a few weeks than I had ever done before. Above all I learnt to function on the highest level without making mistakes, by taking sugar with LSD.

Once the acid had arrived, Ibiza was transformed. Many people took their first trips. Very few took sugar with them and all sorts of strange things happened to them. Soon a fear of acid spread. I explained to everybody who was interested, and no doubt many who were not, that there was nothing to be afraid of if you knew about the sugar. Up until this point in my life I had always assumed that other people could understand things too, if only informed. Now came the baffling experience of finding out that this was not so. They could listen, or look as if they were listening, but they could not understand. Sometimes I thought they could even understand, but they couldn't act on the basis of that understanding. We cannot all be great original thinkers, but you would think we could all be ordinary understanders. Now I know it is a lack of faith in their own powers of reasoning that makes most people unable to accept a new explanation. They must first have the nod from their accepted authorities, then they will believe. They can't listen, understand, test, check and then know for certain that what they have heard is correct. At best they give the news a high probability rating and then continue to ignore it. The problem was that the accepted authorities, professors, priests, medical practitioners, princes, prime ministers, presidents or whatever, had never heard of this and even if they had heard about it they would have to have taken acid to verify it, which, in the dark age we live in, was not likely to happen!

After a few weeks' experience I was able to carry on a normal life on acid. I would take a trip at any time in any place. I always had a supply of vitamin C tablets in my pocket to keep my adrenal glands full, so I was proof against slipping lower into sugarlack than the level at which adrenalin is automatically secreted to stimulate the liver into releasing more glucose into the blood. This is safety measure number one. It is important to know that the body does not store vitamin C as it does other vitamins. Once saturated it gets rid of any surplus in the urine. On LSD, with the continuous use of adrenalin to counter the sugarlack, the body soon runs out of ascorbic acid (vitamin C), which is used up in the continuously needed production of adrenalin to keep the adrenal glands full. The dangerous part of LSD taking comes when the adrenalin supply is exhausted. Then the sugar level falls below that at which normal brain functions can be maintained. As long as you have adrenalin your sanity is not at risk. You may have a bumpy trip, because of course constant adrenalin secretion brings with it associations of past "fight, fright or flight" situations and these images in their turn trigger the adrenal reflex again and in this way a vicious circle of "horrors" can set in. The only way out of this is to take some sugar. Raising the bloodsugar level above the adrenal point keeps the mind clear and alert and concentrated on the present and future, rather than the past. Having said this, I will not deny that the regression of sugarlack can be useful in the psycho-analytic sense. The important thing is to know that sugarlack is a lack of sugar in the blood and that taking sugar will raise you above it. Then you are your own master. The terrifying part of a sugarlack is the apparent reality of the experience together with the sense of eternity or permanence. Knowing that you can bring it to an end can give you the courage to endure it and perhaps, being objective about it, to derive some benefit from it.

With knowledge of the safety measures, sugar and vitamin C, you are ultimately in control of your trip. You take the acid, you can take the sugar. Without that knowledge you take the trip and then get taken for a ride. You are at its mercy, like a boat without a rudder on a flood tide. Many people will say that that is just what they are after – they don't want to be in control. There's too much control in life they say. Of course they are talking about adult life. It is the tragedy of the adult that his self-control is maintained at the expense of his freedom of action. This is because certain parts of the brain, in many cases the sexual centres, are kept under repression so that the Ego can keep his speech centres full of blood. The Ego's grip on the brain is chronic. He can never escape it except by increasing his brainbloodvolume. So he gets high, but usually with the wrong drugs, and is then so poisoned that he cannot use his freedom.

Whilst alcohol is a most enjoyable drug and drinking such a useful social lubricant, drinking too much results in amnesia and ultimately unconsciousness. Heroin is for killing pain. Alcohol and heroin are toxic, addictive drugs. The body produces anti-toxins, which crave the toxins on withdrawal. Freedom in exchange for slavery is no sort of deal. LSD and marijuana are non-toxic. Taking them is remembering. The danger of LSD (and to a far lesser extent pot) lies in the sugarlack that results. With toxic drugs there is an inevitable increase of the dose as the user gets accustomed to them. They need more to get the same result. That is not the case with the non-toxic drugs. No matter how long you have taken them, the same amount will always produce the same result.

With all the brain centres amply supplied with blood there is no need for repression. The function of all the centres is improved by a higher sugar level. Certain consciousness-expanding drugs, such as mescaline and psilocybin, act on the liver in a similar way to adrenalin and with these two you do not need so much extra sugar for top enjoyment. Sugarlack was grossly overvalued by the LSD gurus. It gave them the power of presiding over groups of bewildered novices. Ego-loss became the rage. LSD was a mystery, therefore anything you said about it should be mysterious too. Anything simple and factual was contemptuously disregarded. It was a mystical experience, a union with the cosmic soul, a death and a rebirth, a religious ritual etc – the old words of proven potency were dragged out of the cupboard. These things may be true, but they don't really explain anything. Jung was deified, not Freud. But it was the death fling of the superstitions. Myths were science when they were created. Language evolves, like everything else. We must use today's vocabulary today. The eternal truths remain, but the ways of expressing them evolve, becoming more precise and less ambiguous, calling more for proof and less for belief. The true information about acid wasn't given a chance. Ignorance and superstition won the field but lost the cause. The whole movement collapsed into chaos and anarchy.

On Ibiza people were freaking and flipping out left, right and centre. Perhaps this is a good moment to clear up the acid terminology: freaking out is losing control of your mind on a temporary basis, flipping out is more of a permanent problem. You can freak out on a trip and still be fine the next day, but when you flip out you stay flipped. Your Ego is lost. There's no captain on the ship.

One night I saw a party in progress in an apartment and decided to join it. As I entered the door I caught the eye of an attractive blonde on the far side of the room. The room was full of dancing and drinking couples, but unerringly, as if guided by remote control, the two of us threaded our way towards the same spot, our eyes locked on each other's. I was on acid, needless to say. "What is it? said the girl. "It's a little pill", I replied. It turned out that that had nothing to do with it. Marlies, a French girl, had been born on the same day as me. It is undeniable that there was something that attracted us mutually in a way I have not experienced before or since. Marlies was on holiday with her husband and two children. I told her all about acid and she wanted to try it. I agreed to turn her on and we arranged to meet two days later in a café in town. She was going to see someone off on the boat, then we would take the trip. I told her on no account to have any alcohol to drink beforehand. Subsequently I found out that she had.

I should not have taken it as casually as I did. This was the first person I had turned on to acid and as a result of the experience I realised that the setting is important for the first trip. Privacy is vital, at least until the trip is well under way. The outside world can have an unsettling effect, which is why the Leary school devised their "set and setting" method. They did not give vitamin C and sugar, but relied on the guru shepherding the novice through the trip with quiet words of wisdom. It is a fact that with low bloodsugar a person is highly suggestible, so the words of the guru are lent added power in such a situation. Thereafter he will be revered by his sheep. With sugar-taking none of this is necessary. The guru need only eat sugar himself to show the way (I need hardly say, need I, that sugar comes in many forms, honey, halva, fruit, whatever). The tripper can then look after him or herself.

Anyway Marlies and I met at the café. "Have you got it with you?" she asked. "Yes", I replied. "Let's have it then". I gave it to her there and then. I encouraged her to take some sugar with it and keep taking it, as I did. As the effect came on she began to get a bit nervous and said she would like to see her husband and friends, who were at a restaurant down the road. We went to find them. They had been drinking a lot and were on a completely different wavelength. They kept asking her silly questions and she began to get confused. Her husband was hostile to me and she got into a panic and began to cry. Everyone was shouting and the chaotic scene couldn't have been worse for her. Her husband decided to take her home. Feeling responsible for her, I went with them and tried to explain to the husband that she should keep taking some sugar. Understandably he didn't want to hear me, see me or have anything to do with me. Look what I had done to his poor wife with my drugs. He slammed the door of their house in my face. I went to Marlies's American girlfriend, Pat, and explained the situation to her. She was intelligent and understood that Marlies should eat some sugar. She went round and persuaded her to take some. Within half an hour she was laughing and having a good time; however, she had had an hour or two of hell and didn't want to repeat the experience. I decided never to try such impromptu turning-ons in future.

There were many extraordinary happenings on Ibiza that summer of '65. Fritz walked off the jetty onto a passenger ship as it was casting off, gazing at the sky and repeating the words "love", "truth" and "beauty" one after the other in an endless cycle. Later, in London, I saw a girl doing the same thing, repeating "yesterday is today is tomorrow is yesterday..." and so on as she walked round in a circle. This circular repetition of associated words is the last remnant of Ego maintenance. Fritz was never seen on the island again.

Nick, a painter, and his friend John were living in Solange's mother's house while she was away. When she was due back and Solange gave them notice of this, they didn't want to leave. Solange received a note which said, "It is God's will that Nick and John stay in your mother's house". Strangely enough Solange was taking this seriously and she showed me the note with a worried face. I laughed and tore it up. Nick and John had freaked out together. They had long queues of people lining up to be turned on. They didn't tell people that it was placebo acid (tapwater) and it was a great success. Soon after that Nick started flipping. First he stopped talking altogether, then he gave away all his possessions, including his passport, and silently refused to take them back. One day I saw that he had a watch on and asked him the time. He took the watch off and gave it to me. I said I didn't want it, but he waved me away, so I gave it to the person next to me. On another occasion someone just arrived on the island was asking me where to score. We were in a bar. I looked round the bar and saw Nick in a corner. I told the stranger to hang on and went over to ask Nick if he would sell the man some hash. He had a roomful of it which he had brought back from Pakistan. Without speaking, Nick put his hand in his pocket and pulled out a huge lump of hash. He handed it to me. How much? No, no, shake of the head. I took the hash back to the stranger and gave it to him. How much? Nothing, I said, he gave it to you. He thought for a minute he had really arrived in Paradise.

In the end Nick stopped eating and drinking too, as well as talking, and stood for days on a balcony in someone's apartment, staring out to sea. Then one moment he walked off. Later he was picked up by the police as he was throwing stones at buildings and taken to a mental hospital in Mallorca. After three weeks there, with electric shock treatment, he was released. He came back, talking again and painting, but not taking acid.

Towards the end of the summer a gang of New York youngsters arrived on motorbikes, with leather jackets, boots and knives, the "Wild Ones", don't you know. They called themselves the "Acid Gang" and the star was Acid-King David (later to attain notoriety as the man who supplied the drugs when Mick Jagger was busted at Keith Richard's house in the country, with Marianne Faithfull in nothing but a fur coat). They brought a lot of acid with them and a mythology of knockout trips of more acid than anyone had ever taken (typically American), 10,000 micrograms at a time

(250 was the normal dose) as well as heroin, cocaine etc etc. LSD acts by constricting the neck veins, which causes the capillaries in the brain to swell. The pressure thus created is exerted on the volume of csf in the brain and some of it is squeezed out through the nerve channels, making room for more blood. Taking more than enough to do the trick may get you there quicker, through a stronger constriction, but it will not get you any higher. Just enough gets you as high as you can get, so using more is a waste of good acid.

I felt the time had come to move out of Luciano's house. I was boring him with all my talk of brainbloodvolume, sugarlack etc. I did bang on about it, because I thought it vital that I pass on the information, whatever people thought about me. I foresaw that people were going to get into all sorts of trouble if they took acid in ignorance.

My money had run out earlier than I had expected, the way it does. The Acid Gang received me hospitably and for some time I slept on a sofa in their house. Once Acid-King David threatened me with a knife if I ever mentioned sugar again. I laughed and said he was on a sugarlack. They were nice, the Acid Gang, but nowhere. One of them recounted an hallucination he'd had on acid with heroin. He had been kneeling in the nave of a great cathedral, with massed choirs of angels and archangels soaring up on either side. Then out of a brilliant, blinding white light came the voice of God the Father offering him the secrets of the universe, and he was afraid and said no thank you. Oh dear!

In November, when I had thoroughly digested all this new information I had received and Bart had also explained to me and Fran his discovery of the Ego mechanism, which completed the knowledge, I felt that it was time to turn myself loose on London. There, I thought, I will find intelligent, well-educated people who will understand what I am talking about. They will be only too pleased to ask Bart over to lecture to the Royal Society and from there we will approach the government and get them to distribute the information free before the acid explosion takes place. England will become Aldous Huxley's *Island*. With the information the people will be ready for the acid when it comes. That is one thing about acid-taking; hope springs eternal. One can see what must happen and takes the optimistic view. In retrospect I can see that it was foolish, but at the time I thought it was just a matter of seeing the right people. So it would have been, no doubt, if only they existed.

It was obvious to all of us on Ibiza that summer that acid was going to spread like wildfire. In the autumn the egg broke and out burst the evangelists, people splitting from the island in all directions, carrying the good tidings. Acid-King David gave me some money to get off the island. He was keen to see the back of me I think. I told Bart that I would arrange lectures for him in London and send him a ticket when it was all fixed up. Having arrived six months earlier in a desperate position, I was now leaving with a direction to head in for my whole life. I had arrived empty. I left full.

I took the boat across to Barcelona. John Doyle and his wife Monique were also on it. Monique had translated the scroll into French. There were also several others that I knew on the voyage. It was a very rough night. Many people were very sick. In Barcelona I stayed for a few days with some friends of John and Monique and made the acquaintance of two attractive German sisters. We went to a concert given by the American Folk and Blues Artists. It was in a high-roofed theatre and we were sitting near the top. The audience consisted largely of Spanish students. There was something rather grim about the way they all looked the same. All had crew-cuts, white shirts and ties with no jackets. At intervals in each row there were seated slightly older-looking ones with shades on. After a bit it became clear that these were the authorities. Spain was still in the grip of the Franco dictatorship at that time.

The concert began with a solitary black man sitting on a chair in the middle of the stage. I could sense the hostility of the audience. The singer tapped the boards slowly with his foot. The beat began to establish itself. After a minute or so he picked a few notes on his guitar, then some chords, and the rhythm built up. At last he started singing. His voice rang through the theatre as he sang the blues, but the audience didn't respond at all. At the end of his magnetic performance there was some unenthusiastic applause. I could see that it was quite a test for the singers.

Next on was Big Mama Johnson. That broke the ice. During

her first number some members of the audience couldn't resist a spontaneous cheer and they began to tap their feet in time to the music. At once the shaded authorities set up a violent hissing which swept along the rows and silenced the response. The same thing happened several more times. It was the most obvious glimpse of fascism in action I had seen. I couldn't see what they had against the audience participating and creating a happy atmosphere. I think they must have been afraid of things getting out of their control.

As I had no money, I decided to go to the British Consulate and get the rail fare to England in exchange for my passport, which would be returned on repayment. On the train was Lloyd Bridges, a negro poet from the USA, whom I had met in Barcelona. He was going to Paris. We passed the journey pleasantly talking and before he left he gave me an ounce of grass wrapped in some newspaper. I carried on to Calais and caught the boat for Dover. I put the grass at the bottom of a basket which contained some food and a pen and paper.

As I was passing onto the boat I noticed that one very fuzz-like character slipped to the front of the queue and then went down some stairs past a notice saying "No Admission". He could have passed for a tourist with shades except for his suspicious behaviour. I was on acid, so I noticed these things. Still, I wasn't worried. Why should they be after me? Or could that poet have set me up? It was a beautiful day. I stood in the stern as the boat left Calais, watching the seagulls trying vainly to keep up with the ship against the slipstream. I was excited as the white cliffs of Dover came into view. England here I come, I thought; you are my Island.

While I was waiting in the queue to show passports to the officials (in my case a bit of paper), I felt a tap on my shoulder and, looking round, saw a be-mackintoshed plain-clothes man smiling at me in a knowing way. "Mr Mellen", he said, "would you mind coming this way please?". He led me into a room and asked various questions: where had I come from? Why? Where was I going to? etc etc. I answered him patiently. Then he asked me if I would mind having my baggage searched. "Not at all", I said, "Go ahead." I had a small suitcase full of dirty clothes and the basket with some bits of bread and carrot in. He rummaged through it all, not bothering to look beneath the carrots where I had put the marijuana. I was relieved. For a moment I had been quite worried. It occurred to me that no one in the world knew where I was at that exact time. I could have disappeared for ever and no one would have been any the wiser. After his fruitless search the knowing cop said I could go. He looked as if he had stepped off the set of one of those pre-war Ealing comedies, with a little RAF-type moustache and all. How do they get to be like that I wondered. It was not an auspicious start to my return to England.

In London I borrowed a pound from Martin and put it on a horse called "On The Mat". It won at 33-1. That was better. Martin and Suna had split up and he was living in a flat belonging to Amanda Feilding, a spacious flat on the top floor of a house overlooking the river in Chelsea. In Ibiza I had met Michael Brody, an American actor with the Living Theatre, who was travelling round the world. We had become friends and I had given him Martin's address to look up in London. Now I found him there ensconced with Amanda. Amanda was a beautiful and eccentric sculptress, usually flying high on LSD or speed. Michael sat quietly beside her, lighting one pipe after another. The flat was a centre for all the lunatics in London, popstars, artists, speedfreaks, junkies, smokers and acid-heads. Amanda herself was usually too stoned to get up off the bed, where she reclined like an Egyptian sphinx-queen, surveying the havoc around her with eyes like black searchlights. I can remember the scene well. There was a continuous buzz of talk – conversation was too good a word for it – as everyone spoke at the same time. Amanda hardly ever said a word, but she tuned in to whatever the various people were saying and, as she caught their eye, made the appropriate expressions to signal her understanding, sympathy, amusement, amazement or whatever.

Michael Rainey was starting a psychedelic clothes shop called "Hung On You", where all the pop stars bought their clothes. He took me round to a flat in Cadogan Lane. The tenants were four teenage girls, Liz, Charlotte, Julia and Fiona, and they occupied the four beds. The sitting room housed at times up to fourteen homeless males sleeping all over the floor and sofas. I moved in and within a short time was sharing Liz's bed. Liz was graceful, tall, dark and intelligent. She was also witty and I enjoyed her company very much. I pinned the scroll up on the wall and, having found John Doyle, who had found some acid, I was soon in business. Cadogan Lane became one of the happiest turn on centres there's ever been. Many people came there and took acid. I always gave them sugar with it. I don't think anyone had a bad trip. However, turning people on is one thing and teaching them the mechanism is another. No one really understood what I was telling them about increased brainbloodvolume and intra-cranial pressure. It was just the same as in Ibiza.

John Doyle told me that I should go and see Michael Hollingshead, who had been on the Leary scene in America. He didn't understand the mechanism, but I thought I would give him time for that. On the other hand he did see the importance of acid for the future. It was Michael who had given Tim Leary his first trip, so he was an old-established guru. I didn't like his emphasis on mandalas and mantras and the *Tibetan Book of the Dead* etc. I explained to him that it was all far simpler than he thought. Still he didn't see it. Despite his name, which he had assumed because the highest chakra in the Tantric scale is a hole in the top of the head, he was unfortunately still adult and maintained a sort of equilibrium on acid by taking heroin and other toxic substances with it to depress his brain metabolism. He insisted that the Tantric hole in the head, symbolised by the red dot on the forehead, was just that, a symbol of a state of mind. I would rather have the state of mind than the symbol myself. I don't think he realised that there was anything in what I was saying until I drew the analogy for him between the Ego and the government, pointing out that each is an instrument of repression that keeps the greater part of the available energy for its own use. Now he began to buy sweets and have plates of them all over the house when people were turning on, and he also started eating oranges. Even though he couldn't really understand the mechanism, he could tell that I knew what I was talking about and my self-mastery on acid was clear proof of the effectiveness of my method.

Michael had an apparently inexhaustible supply of acid. His function was simply to distribute it. I told him that the open letter explaining the mechanism (which Bart had written to the Professor of Psycho-Analysis and Psychiatry at Amsterdam University) should be given to every dealer to safeguard against flip-outs. He got the letter reproduced in hundreds and we began distributing them. Michael and his friend Desmond O'Brien had set up "The World Psychedelic Centre" in a luxurious flat in Pont Street. Desmond was the financier and Michael the guru. Michael came round to Cadogan Lane and was very impressed by the happy scene he found there, lots of young people on acid with no one putting over a big mystery scene. This was something new to him. His "sessions" were always in a darkened room smelling of incense, with a slide show of mandalas and a commentary by the guru. That was the way the Americans had devised to keep people in control. It was not my idea of a good time. However, the World Psychedelic Centre was very useful. First they supplied me with all the acid I wanted and later Desmond provided the money to get Bart a ticket from Ibiza and for me to rent a flat in London. Before that happened Cadogan Lane came to an end when the owner discovered what was going on there. There was a big scene and we were all turned out. The girls split up. Liz went down to the country to stay with her parents. I moved into Pont Street and carried on from there.

The World Psychedelic Centre operated on a much bigger scale than Cadogan Lane. There nothing had been planned, it was just one long happening. Pont Street was planned. Michael was hardly ever off the telephone. He gave acid parties and asked famous people. Roman Polanski, Feliks Topolski, Alex Trocchi and others passed through. At one party Paul McCartney of the Beatles turned up. I showed him the scroll and started explaining it to him. He looked puzzled. The friend who had brought him to the party got hostile and started arguing with me, saying that it was not true. It was the threatened guru syndrome again; he was the expert.

I could not make sure that everybody took sugar with their trips. For one thing, Michael used to put acid in the food or drink of girls he wanted to take advantage of under the influence, an unforgivable liberty. People were behaving very strangely all over the place. Taxis were always arriving full of acid freaks and the neighbours in that respectable area must have got very uptight.

Sooner or later there was going to be trouble.

I had the scroll hanging in my room. The routine was that when people came round to take acid John or Michael would bring them in for me to point to the diagrams and explain the methods of increasing the brainbloodvolume which were illustrated. One night I was in my room, relaxing on the bed. There were five or six people next door in the sitting room. John came into my room with two hefty-looking men. I thought there was something a bit strange about them; still, I'll answer their questions on the mechanism – you never know... "Have you got any drugs?" asked one of them in a voice which was definitely not that of a potential student. I realised what had happened. "Yes", I said, pointing to the lump of hash on the table, "there". He picked it up and sniffed it. "You're under arrest", he said.

There were six of them in the flat. Someone had left the front door open and they had let themselves in. They turned the flat upside down. I could hear them breaking things. I went into the hall and asked which one was in authority. He pointed to another. To this one I said quietly that I quite understood that he was just doing his job, but I couldn't see why they shouldn't behave properly while doing it. He told them to take it easy. Now I suggested to them that, as they were here, they might as well take the opportunity to learn about one of the most important discoveries in history. I said I didn't see why the police should be excluded from the knowledge just because they had such an unpleasant job to do. They agreed and I took them all to the scroll and explained the whole thing to them. After that we were all good friends. Apologetically they continued the search. Half-heartedly one of them went through the clothes hanging in the cupboard in my room. I held my breath and he didn't find the small bottle of acid in a coat pocket. They had found three ounces of hash and some other drugs belonging to one of the visitors. Six of us were taken down to the police station to be fingerprinted and charged.

While we were there we had a jolly time, singing songs and joking with the cops. One of them found a rolled joint in the breast pocket of my jacket. I suggested we smoke it. Two or three of them were in favour, but in the end they rejected the idea because they had no authority to do so. I was allowed to ring Martin, who agreed to stand bail for Michael and me. The others fixed their own. After three or four hours we were released. Before we left I said goodbye to my police friends and then added that I envied them, because now that their job was done they could go home and have a drink and a fag. We, on the other hand, didn't drink alcohol and didn't smoke tobacco and now didn't even have any hash to smoke. "You might give us back just a little bit", I said. One of them disappeared and came back with the whole bag full bar a little bit which they kept for analysis and evidence. We thanked them and said goodnight.

The court case came up a few weeks later. We all stood in the dock. I had decided to plead guilty and make a statement. I learnt my short speech by heart. It was built around the passage in the open letter in which Bart had written: "The evolutionary religion protects the right of the individual to have his own blood in his own brain." I elaborated a bit on that and gave a short and clear description of the mechanism of brainbloodvolume. No one else made a statement. When questioned about my income I stated that I had none. I said I would make a collection among my friends to pay the fine. I was fined £20. The rest were fined £50 each. Outside the courtroom one of the coppers said to me, "Here, that was a bit of a spiel you put over, weren't it?". I told him it was true. He didn't think that very likely, judging by the way he winked.

After the bust the Pont Street scene began to crumble. People were afraid to go there. Michael took more and more toxic drugs and his behaviour became very unpredictable. At about that time Desmond gave me some money to send Bart a ticket with. Bart arrived, looking tanned and healthy. It was early 1966 by now. With more money from Desmond I managed to rent a flat in Edith Grove, a street connecting the Fulham Road with the King's Road below World's End. John Doyle and Monique moved in, as also did Bob, a speedfreak from Cadogan Lane, with Fiona, his girlfriend, and soon the flat had become another oasis for the nomadic smoking crowd, with a constant trail of visitors arriving and leaving. A pretty Swedish girl called Eva moved in with Bart, having nowhere else to live. A new routine set in. I arranged for Bart to appear on television. Unfortunately the interview was only shown in the north of England, so we couldn't see it, but it went very well. Then Bart and I gave a talk at Better Books, the avant-garde bookshop. Before that we had been to a poetry reading there, given by a friend of John's called Colin Wilson and my friend from the train, Lloyd Bridges.

Earlier in the year at Pont Street one night a very square-looking character, with a suit and tie on, had come round. He appeared so naïve and yet so interested in the mechanism that I decided to turn him on to acid as he requested. He seemed to have a good time. He gave his name as Joe and said he had missed the last bus back to Richmond, so could he stay the night. Of course he could. He took our hospitality, our acid and our hash and then left, having been well treated. It was soon after that that we were busted.

On the night of the poetry reading Joe turned up at Edith Grove, still besuited and square-looking. He accepted a trip and came with us to the reading, where he made an exhibition of himself. As Colin was reading one of Lloyd's poems he stood up and declared that he could read better than that. Okay, said Colin, come up and read it yourself. Up got Joe, scarlet in the face, and went to the rostrum and read the poem. We looked at each other and shrugged our shoulders. The poor chap was obviously on a sugarlack and making a fool of himself. His reading was no improvement on Colin's and everyone was relieved when it was over. Later I realised that it was a very clever move. It got him accepted as a sort of square freak. Thereafter he came to call quite regularly and often stayed the night. No one paid much attention to him. He just sat around and listened. In retrospect I could make connections between him and Lloyd Bridges and the police search at Dover and the bust at Pont Street and so on, but at the time the last thing I was concerned with was being "infiltrated" by plain-clothes policemen. It was too ridiculous. It wasn't as if I was trying to hide anything. Indeed, earlier in the year, feeling obliged to warn against the dangers of ignorant acid-taking, I had walked into the canteen at Chelsea Police Station at lunch time, when it was full of policemen eating, craved their indulgence while I pinned up the scroll and then asked for their attention. I told them that I expected LSD to become popular in the near future and explained that there were likely to be many casualties. In that event, I said, the essential safety measures were to take sugar and vitamin C, so if they were faced with the situation they would know what to do to bring the victims back to reality. They had listened quietly, if with a shade of bewilderment, before resuming their meal.

By now acid had hit the headlines and the Sunday papers were full of scare stories. John invited the press to a party of Christopher Gibbs in his beautiful flat on Cheyne Walk. It was reported in the most scandalous way. There was a picture of Olivia, a Belgian girl, breastfeeding her baby and a description of this drug-crazed orgy with copulating couples sprawled all over the place amidst the burst bags of sugar! It didn't sound like the party I was at at all. After our lecture at Better Books two nice-talking journalists from *The People* approached me and asked if they could interview Bart. I asked Bart and he agreed. All night long they sat up, asking questions with a tape recorder on. Bart gave them all the answers and explained the mechanism quite clearly. The next day an article appeared headed: "This Dangerous Idiot Should be Thrown Out". Not a word of truth was in it. They reported Bart as advocating self-trepanation, which he most certainly did not. What he had said in the scroll was, "with today's knowledge of operating techniques one could easily do this by oneself". Being a medical student, with this knowledge, he had done it himself after failing to find a doctor to do it for him. Then they quoted a publicity-seeking doctor and an over-ripe Tory MP laying down the law about what should be done with such intolerable creatures. It was disgusting. I went round to the newspaper's office to give a piece of my mind to those journalists who had so deceived us, but of course they were not in. Bart had already experienced the slime of journalese in Amsterdam. Now I found out about it. I decided to try only with respectable papers from now on. I wrote to all of them, asking for a bit of space, but none of them would touch the subject. I was learning a bit more about taboo every day.

On another occasion a BBC television team came to me, asking if I could arrange an acid trip for them to televise. I got about ten people together, including five very attractive girls. The trip was to start in the afternoon. The poet George Andrews agreed to take part with us. The television crew spent an hour or so setting up all their equipment, cameras, lights coils and coils of wire and spools and spools of film. Our flat was too small, so we had gathered at a friend's flat in the Earls Court Road. When the preparations were at last completed they asked us to take the acid. Aware that we were being filmed, I handed each person their trip on a sugarlump and then handed round dishes of Turkish Delight. They asked us questions about how we were feeling now. They were obviously expecting something strange to happen, but they were disappointed. You cannot film what is happening in the brain. Everyone said they felt "high" and "great" and things like that. In fact the trippers were much more interested in what the film crew were doing than vice versa. Bart told them all about the mechanism and I added my bit. George recited some of his poetry and then Dan Richter, another American poet, turned up. He was not on acid, but he could talk about it and for the rest of the time they filmed an interview with him. He was very pleased to have walked in on a starring role and told a lot of weird tales about acid flip-outs while the trippers sat around and enjoyed a sunny afternoon. When the film appeared on TV they showed everyone saying their piece except Bart and me, but the largest slice was Dan Richter's. Since they had wanted to film someone having a bad trip, they later shot some film of four unfortunate people on belladonna, moaning and writhing, and included this as an acid experience.

My opinion of reporters was getting lower and lower. They regarded themselves as the guardians of free speech and the great, objective mediums of information. I saw them as a lot of parasites, getting their kicks vicariously from other people's lives. Still, without the press, how were we to get the news across? By now acid had already got a bad name and every day it got worse. Soon it was made illegal. The dream of England as the paradise island had slipped away. During the summer I wrote an interview with Bart and, having left a strategic copy in Christopher Gibbs's flat, I was pleased to find out that there was someone interested in publishing it. This was Jasper Heathcote Williams, who was working for the *Transatlantic Review*, a literary magazine. He had been at Eton with me and we had once met, in the school boxing competition. He printed the interview and subsequently it was printed several more times in various other publications. Later Jasper wrote a play called *AC/DC*, in which he included a trepanation scene as the climax. The play was very successful and won him an award as the most promising playwright of the year. I also wrote some mechanism songs at that time and Julie Felix, a popular American folk singer, who later had her own TV show, recorded three of them on LPs. Julie had a pretty good understanding of the mechanism and did everything she could to promote it. The songs she recorded were 'Brainbloodvolume', 'The Great Brain Robbery' and 'Sugarlack'.

Later in the spring two reporters from the German magazine *Stern* came to see me. They wanted to take a trip and write about it. I agreed to get them some acid and round up some people to accompany them. Once again I asked the most glamorous female acid-heads to cooperate. The two Germans were extremely nice. One was the writer, the other the photographer. About ten of us took the trips together. After about an hour we decided to go to Battersea Fun Fair. Taking plenty of sweets and vitamin C tablets, we set off in two taxis. By the time we got there we were well and truly high. The writer was particularly struck by the grotesque appearance of many members of the public, something which is very noticeable on a first trip. Werner, the photographer, wanted to go into the House of Mirrors, a maze of distorting mirrors, which was hard enough to get through without acid. In the middle he got hopelessly lost. Whichever way he looked he saw himself twisted and contorted, blown up or elongated, looking at himself in despair. A member of the public came by and Werner appealed to him for help. "I'm lost!" he said. "That's what you paid for" said the man, walking on past him. At last he found his way out. The owner of the House of Mirrors and his wife were standing there in their miniature fairy garden, surrounded by its little fence, a foot high. Werner was about to step over it when something made him stop. Perhaps he should first ask their permission. They were very amused by his unnecessary politeness. At last he caught sight of the rest of us waiting for him. "Thank God", he said as he came up to us, "I was lost and now I'm found again." Bart put a glucose tablet in his mouth and soon he was alright. The rest of the trip went off successfully. Both the Germans had a good time. They stayed in London for a week and spent hours discussing the mechanism in their thorough Teutonic way. We took another trip and went to the zoo. Again they enjoyed themselves very much. By the end of the week it was time for them to leave. They seemed to understand the mechanism completely and we were very optimistic. They even paid us enough for two months' rent for the flat. I excepted them from the run of the mill journalists. They had taken the acid themselves, so they knew what it was all about.

The article appeared a month or two after that. Whilst it was a very positive article and gave a good report of acid, it was disappointing in that not a word about the mechanism was included. They sent us the English version before it appeared in the shops, so we were anticipating its sale with some eagerness. Maybe this would start the ball rolling. However, when it did come out in London, extraordinarily the article had been torn out of every copy, leaving a gap in the page numbers. We went to three different newsagents and it was the same in each case. Rumour had it that Brian Epstein was behind it. Right at the end of the article they had mentioned that several pop groups, including the Beatles, had taken acid. There seemed to be no end to the suppression of the information.

I was running out of newspapers and influential people to send the open letter to. I had sent it to a great many and got only a few replies, all of them negative. The general line was that they couldn't take the responsibility of printing the information without independent medical confirmation. Of course that was never forthcoming, since it was unknown to the medical profession. At that time they were still denying that there could be such a thing as expanded consciousness. Naturally this is something you can only find out by expanding your own consciousness. It is a subjective experience, though maybe the increase of blood volume can be observed as an objective fact with modern scanning techniques. I don't know if they can measure the capillary volume in the brain – I suppose it's a bit unlikely in fact, considering there must be billions of capillaries in a space smaller than a football! Whilst the doctors were admitting that they did not know the action of LSD, long books on the subject were appearing with rows of letters after the authors' names. Their attitude towards the mechanism was extremely superior, as if they were too all-knowing to be told anything new. In my opinion expanded consciousness is not a medical matter at all. The mechanism of brainbloodvolume is the first scientific explanation of the central religious, or mystical, experience. Here again there is probably some confusion in the medical mind. Doctors are a paternalistic lot. It reminds me of the old Oxford joke about some Americans being shown around the university. On either side of Turl Street stand the colleges of Lincoln and Jesus. The guide mixed up which was which and then apologised. "That's alright," said one of the Americans, "we often make the same mistake".

Despite the failure of our attempts to spread the news, life went on pleasantly. Many wandering acid-heads passed through and picked up a few new words. An American girl called Barbara, an old friend of Bart's, came by and stayed for a while in the flat. To begin with I was attracted to her and she shared my bed. She was planning a mammoth psychedelic movie, the main point of which was to include every famous person "on the scene" from Jean Genet to Bob Dylan and the Stones. She had made a list of all the people and was travelling the world to interview them. Bart was one of them, hence the visit. The movie script was not as long as the list of stars, but Barbara kept a precarious Ego maintained by talking about it all day long. In the end the non-stop nonsense got too much and I turned her out. She refused to go, so I put her baggage outside the front door. Finally she went, but she paid me back by stealing quite a bit of acid first.

Soon after Bart arrived in London there was a party at Christopher Gibbs's flat and Amanda Feilding, who had been in the country for a time recovering from hepatitis, came back to London for the party, where she met Bart. Michael Brody had left the country. Bart strongly fancied Amanda and soon moved into her flat on Chelsea Embankment. I carried on in Edith Grove. One night, returning from a visit to the Embankment, I found that the flat had been broken into and turned upside down. I noticed that the hash pipe had been taken, but nothing else. I concluded that it must have been the fuzz again. Luckily they hadn't found the acid. I was surprised that they had simply broken down the door to get in, but after all they are only playing cops and robbers on the right side of the law. The next day they came around and charged me with possession of a pipe in which traces of cannabis resin had been found. There is no end to their cleverness. It was about this time that several other flats on the circuit were busted. It turned out that the square freak, Joe, had played the same scene in other flats as in mine. He had missed the last bus to Richmond and stayed the night and so on. He finally broke his cover by visiting Amanda's flat with a colleague who took out a note pad and started jotting down answers to impertinent questions. It made us laugh, but it also made us angry. I wondered if he had really taken the acid I had given him. Probably not, but he had certainly smoked our hash.

It was all so stupid. I mean we were not anti-social criminals. On the contrary we were bringing the message of love and understanding, which can transform society into something more enjoyable than it is at present. As technology evolves and the need for long working hours is reduced, the filling of leisure hours will become more of a priority and it is in this department that expanded consciousness will come into its own. It restores the creativity and enthusiasm of youth to the adult. It brings the realisation that love and health are greater aims than money and power. Whilst the means of providing for the material needs of man have in the main been discovered, his mental or "spiritual" needs are much farther from being satisfied. In my opinion man's greatest need was to have more blood in his brain, to escape the straightjacket of the Ego. Still, my immediate problem was having been found in possession of some hash ash. I realised that I could go to prison for this, as it would be my second offence. The case was postponed for weeks, as usual, and I remained free on bail.

Things weren't looking so bright. I had no money to pay the rent with. As with Pont Street, the bust frightened people off and the Edith Grove scene was collapsing. Amanda kindly let me stay in a room in her flat. She and Bart were planning to go on a visit to Amsterdam. I planned to trepan myself while they were away.

It was August 1966. For some time I had been contemplating getting trepanned. Magically I was well-prepared for it by the coincidence of my mother having a large crater in her forehead. She had fallen over a cliff when she was eight and smashed her head on the rocks below. Her father had climbed down the cliff and saved her life by carrying her back on his shoulders and getting her to hospital on time. My only concern was HOW to get trepanned. To begin with the idea of doing it myself seemed out of the question. This was where the doctors could come in useful. I made some enquiries and found out that they were not prepared to do it without some indication, ie some condition to cure. I explained that the condition was adulthood, a brain without pulsation, but they thought that was ridiculous. Adulthood was no known disease. I said whether you called it a disease or not was beside the point: there was still a loss that could be recovered. They had never heard anything like that and there were no books they could look it up in.

By now I was so accustomed to the state of expanded consciousness that the thought of life without it was inconceivable. I was so aware of the benefits of it that the chance to make it permanent in any degree was one I could not miss. I had not known Bart before his operation, but I believed him when he said it made a difference and I understood the explanation of why it did. Without actually having the hole and knowing from experience I had to act in some degree on faith. I thought of asking Bart to trepan me, but I knew he didn't want to be involved in other people's trepanations. He had been tricked into entering a mental hospital after his own operation and kept there for three weeks against his will. If they could do that to him for drilling a hole in his own skull, how much worse might their reaction be to his drilling a hole in someone else's? Gradually I realised that this was my problem and I would have to solve it myself.

Understanding how a hole in the skull results in an increase in the volume of blood in the brain capillaries is the most difficult part of the whole thing. Everyone can see the pulsation under the separate pieces of the new born baby's skull. It is the same pulse that can be felt at the wrist or anywhere else outside the skull if pressure is applied to an artery, the expansion in the bloodvessels following the heartbeat. After thinking about it Bart concluded that this pulsation in the brain was suppressed by the sealing of the skull at the end of growth and that making a hole in the skull would restore it. The pulsepressure in the brain's arteries would force csf out of the brain, leaving blood in its place. Consciousness would be expanded again, restored to the childhood level.

Man has a longer growth period than any other animal, around twenty one years. It is in this period that the great bulk of his learning is done. Man's survival in competition with the wild animals that hunt on the plain owes a lot to the use he has made of his extra period of youth and learning ability. The great use he makes of his mental powers, the ability to rehearse actions in his imagination and think ahead, has compensated for the inferiority of his natural physical powers compared to other predators. In the struggle for survival thinking is man's trump card. Speech evolved with the increased size of the brain which coincided with standing upright. It became the dominant part of behaviour and set the human being apart from his ape cousins.

What Bart was the first person to see was that standing in the upright position meant that gravity was pulling on the blood in the brain. Compared with an animal on four legs, whose neck is horizontal with his heart, he will lose blood, which is heavier than csf. This is bad enough, but worse is to follow.

The speech centres are the last of the major brain centres to have been established and are situated high up in the cortex, as far away from the heart as can be. With the further loss of blood which follows the sealing of the skull their very survival is threatened. Naturally they would be the last centres to be reached by the blood and therefore the first parts to suffer from the deprivations of gravity. As a result of this another mechanism has evolved to ensure that they are kept supplied with blood.

Think of a sponge with not enough water to saturate it; by squeezing one part dry you will concentrate the water in the other part. It was Bart's insight that this is what happens in the brain and the Ego is the agent responsible for doing the squeezing, by means of the grip which it has on the brain's arteries.

The recognition of the word's meaning, in the listening centre, is the stimulus for the arteries leading to other parts of the brain to be constricted, so that blood can be concentrated in the talking centre, for another word to be spoken, then recognised and so on. One word leads to another. A chain of associated words establishes and maintains priority in the distribution of blood to the speech centres. A closed circuit is formed between the talking and the listening centres. It is a conditioned reflex mechanism. Word recognition is the conditioned stimulus. The

Ego has the power to repress function in a particular part of the brain by constricting the arteries leading to it, thus cutting off its blood supply. This is the physiological basis of repression. The problems arise when repression (usually infantile) becomes chronic and leads to neurosis. When a part of the brain becomes "frozen", as it were, and blocked off from function, any impulses that would normally go to it are diverted and behaviour becomes distorted. This is what Freud saw in his patients. What he didn't see was the physiological basis of it. His "Project for a Scientific Psychology", still considered a seminal work today, attempted to explain it in terms of electrical activity in the central nervous system, but in the end he gave up the attempt.

Bart realised that the damage done by the sealing of the skull, the resulting loss of brainblood, could be reversed by making a hole in it, to allow the membranes around the brain to expand on the heartbeat and set the pulsation off again. It's a bit like a drum membrane reverberating when the drum is struck. With the extra pulsepressure (the difference between the diastolic and systolic pressure) blowing them up, the brain capillaries would contain an additional volume of blood, the volume that had drained away when the pulsation was suppressed and the capillaries had shrunk. With the sealing of the skull the ratio between the volumes of blood and csf had changed, blood decreasing and csf increasing. Making a hole would reverse this change. With the restoration of the pulsation the capillaries are blown up again and the pulsepressure forces out of the brain as much csf as must be displaced by the additional blood.

It is important to remember that it is all a question of the volume of blood contained in the brain capillaries. These are the tiniest bloodvessels of all. It is from them that the brain cells take their glucose and oxygen, which they combust to do their work. With a greater surface area of contact between the brain cells and the capillaries, more oxygen and glucose can be taken from the blood and more carbon dioxide (the waste product of brain metabolism) can be washed away by it. This increased brain metabolism (the oxidation of glucose) means an improvement of function. More energy (consciousness) is produced. Subjectively it is experienced as highly enjoyable.

While in England Bart had met an old friend from Amsterdam, who had, years before, taught him the art of colouring antique prints. He ᵥ   now a partner in one of the largest print shops in London and wᵥ   ᵗᵒ to give Bart some work to do. Bart coloured away and had soon ᵥ   ᵈ quite a bit of money, enough to buy the hand trepan which wᵥ   ˢeen in the surgical instrument shop. It looked something like a   ᵇscrew, only with a ring of teeth at the bottom of the stem. Into thᵢ.   ᵞᵍ, about a centimetre deep, fitted a cylindrical piece of steel with a ᵨ   ᵗᵗ on. This point was used to make the first impression on the skull, ᵥ ˙ idea being that when it had gone in a millimetre or two the ring of teeth would start biting. Once they had made a good groove, the point was removed and the rest of the boring was done with the ring of teeth. When right through the bone, owing to the fact that the ring was narrowest at the bottom, the piece of bone (rondel) would be removed and come out with the trepan. Bart himself had used an electric drill, but I could not afford one at that time and anyhow the hand trepan had the advantage of not needing power, thus avoiding the risk of electrical failure or power cut during the operation. I asked Bart all the questions I could think of on the details of how to do it, including the precautions to take, how to sterilise the instruments etc. Once I had the instructions written down I could practise in my own time. Amanda agreed to let me stay in her flat to do it there. She and Bart were planning a trip to Amsterdam.

Looking back on it now, I can see that I made the characteristic mistake of going ahead before I was really prepared. I would have done better to wait for a year and get thoroughly used to the idea. As it was, my younger brother personality made me force myself to overcome the dread of doing it far too soon. After Amanda and Bart had left I set about preparing everything. I was expecting them back within a week or two and I wanted to do it while they were away. Then no one could accuse Bart of having done it and I would take all the credit myself. It felt like a battle between me and gravity and old man gravity is a crafty opponent. I stopped smoking hash for three days, so as to be well and truly able to feel the going up. Then, on the day I had planned, a Sunday, I started.

I had never given myself an injection before. That sort of thing was not for me. Frankly I considered it disgusting, like all surgery. On Bart's advice I had bought very thin needles. Having shaved a patch of hair off the top of my head, in the middle of the crown, I now began to inject the local anaesthetic. The needles were much too thin; they were not much thicker than 5 amp fusewire and they simply curled up and broke. This is ridiculous I thought. If only I could do it on acid it would be so simple. No sooner had I thought of that than I had decided on it. Okay, so I wouldn't feel the lift up, but so what? Whether I felt it happening or not it would still happen and then I would be back on the plateau of youthful energy and enthusiasm for life.

The next day I got some new needles, good short, thick ones that wouldn't bend too much. I took a trip and went to work with some glucose tablets. The injecting was much easier. It took some time, since it was necessary to inject three layers, of skin, muscle and membrane over the skull. Finally I had a lump on top of my head the size of a pullet's egg. Then I used the scalpel to cut through to the bone and make an opening for the introduction of the trepan. It was now that my difficulties began. The point on the end of the centrepiece was so blunt that it made no impression on the bone. That was something I hadn't bargained on. I tried using the trepan without the centrepiece, but the teeth wouldn't grip the bone without the central pivot. For two hours I struggled to get the damned thing to start cutting, but to no avail. I realised that it would need quite some force applied from on top to get the centrepiece digging into the bone. There was absolutely no pain in the head but it was a pain in the butt. Doing it by oneself was rather like trying to uncork a bottle from inside it. I was very disappointed. I had felt fine, without fear, and had been very keen to get through by myself without help, but it was impossible. I rang Bart in Amsterdam and told him what had happened. I said I would need his help to get the trepan gripping the bone; thereafter I could do it on my own. Bart was coming back in a day or two and he agreed to help. It was now that I made another decision which I was to regret in the future. I decided to tell a lie and announce to the press and grapevine that I had done it on that day, so that Bart would be protected from insinuations by the date stamped in his passport. I rang two or three journalists and gave them the news. Two of them interviewed me with a bandage on my head and then went off to write articles about it.

As it turned out the articles were suppressed, so the news did not appear in the daily papers, though later one of the underground newspapers carried three lines about it.

Gravity had won the battle so far and now it played another ace. Bart was refused entry to the country and Amanda came back without him. What should I do now? I had a great wound in my head. It seemed stupid to cancel the attempt at this stage. Amanda agreed to help me. I cannot praise her too highly for her courage and coolness in an emergency. I can certainly say that no one else would have done it and indeed there was no one else that I could consider asking. However, Amanda is someone apart from the rest and she agreed to help without hesitation.

Once again I took a trip before going to work and once again things didn't go as planned. Amanda was rotating the trepan, pressing with all her might on the point on the top of my head as I knelt in front of a mirror. Eventually the teeth got a grip and the real boring could begin. From now on I could do it alone. After a while, as I was removing the trepan for a rest, thinking I must be nearly through by now, I suddenly felt a kind of mist rising inside me, which quickly spread over the brain and blanketed my consciousness. I felt the strength drain away from my limbs and I sank weakly to the floor, only just conscious and unable to speak above a whisper. I must say that I was scared. What had happened? I didn't know. I supposed I had fainted, perhaps through loss of blood. Whatever it was, I was now "hors de combat". Amanda rang a doctor friend, who rang an ambulance and within half an hour I was on my way to hospital, having been given a largactyl. Amanda came with me in the ambulance and, as I was being wheeled through the white-coated corridors of Emergencies, it was good to see her following the procession.

I was soon feeling alright again. I was put in a spare bed in the Ear, Nose and Throat ward. That in itself was an experience – what some poor people suffer! The wheezing and coughing and excruciating throat-clearing were more than I could have imagined. Amanda saw me installed before leaving and promised to come back with some books for me to read. By now I was feeling pretty foolish. Here I was, feeling perfectly well, in bed in hospital, the heart of the "enemy's" camp. The nurses were lovely. Their noble profession makes them beautiful people. The doctors came prowling round every so often in small groups, looking very seriously at charts on the bottom of the bed, then making some putting down remarks. Their general advice was not to try it again. I told them I was going to, unless they would be good enough to finish the job for me. Here I was, in hospital; ten minutes in the operating theatre, it would be so simple. That they refused to do. The rule is that there must be an "indication" for an operation, ie a reason to do it. They could not see one; adulthood is not a disease in their book. Not a disease, no, but a disadvantage. Well then, I said, I have no choice. I explained the mechanism to quite a few of them, but they shook their heads wisely, as if to say they knew so much better than I did that it wasn't worth arguing about. One young student seemed to follow the explanation quite well. At the end he said, "your logic seems irrefutable, but I think you're mistaken". The only one who didn't take the superior attitude was a young female student with red hair. She seemed genuinely interested and I promised to send her the open letter when I got home, which I did.

I had a visit from an older female, who was Doctor Dally's assistant. Dr Dally was the psychiatrist. His assistant was a humourless woman who fired questions at me like a Gestapo interrogator, about my family background, my schooling, jobs etc etc. I answered them all and the scowling lady left. I had been in hospital three days and had ploughed through Bertrand Russell's *History of Western Philosophy* and Virginia Woolf's *The Waves* when I was told that once Dr Dally had seen me I could leave. I wondered how long I would have to dally for Dally. It was another couple of days before he appeared. He was a nice man. He asked me if I would mind appearing later in front of a group of psychiatrists, to answer their questions, "a sort of third degree" he said. I said I was quite willing to do that, thinking that it would be an opportunity to enlighten at least one of them while doing it. Dr Dally took my address and phone number and said he would contact me when the time came.

I had been in hospital five days and during that time I was supposed to have been in court to be tried for possession of hash ash. I had a visit from two of the policemen who had broken into my flat. They were nice and amazed at what I had done. I told them that unfortunately it had been a failure. The court case was postponed for a week. Finally I left hospital. It had been an interesting experience. I had talked to quite a few doctors. They ignored the explanation that I gave them. They all said the same thing: I was lucky to be alive and would be mad to try it again.

Back at the Embankment I prepared for my trial. I had hoped to have the third eye before I went to prison – indeed that was another reason for having wanted to do it in a hurry – but that was not to be. In court I said I couldn't deny that the pipe had been in my possession. The magistrate ordered me to be remanded in custody for a week for a probation officer's and psychiatrist's report. I was taken to Brixton in the "meat wagon", the large white van used for transporting prisoners. It consists of two rows of cramped iron cells, one on each side, with one-way blackened windows, through which I could see people going about their business in the streets, though they couldn't see me confined inside. The juxtaposition of these two worlds separated by a membrane of glass and steel brought home the fact that one's freedom had been removed, just the freedom to do the most mundane things, like cross the road to go to the supermarket or wait for a bus.

So here I was in a real prison. It was just like the movies, that high, echoing building with iron staircases and rows of cells one above the other, and the clank of the jailor's keys and all. I had a cell to myself, just like Eton. Davy Graham, the folk and blues singer, whom I had known in Spain and Ibiza, was there too, for driving without insurance. He told me he would always remember his meeting with Bart, who had said to him: "there's only one thing to be afraid of and that's gravity; it brings you down". I wrote him a detailed description of the mechanism of brainbloodvolume on Her Britannic Majesty's toilet paper (the legend "this is the property of Her Britannic Majesty's Government" was printed on every sheet – bad thinking when you consider the use it is most commonly put to). There were a few books knocking around to read, Southey's *Life of Nelson* for some strange reason among others, but the time passed slowly. I thought to myself what shall I do? Shall I say I do smoke hash and intend to go on smoking it, or not? If I do, then I will probably get a few months. If I don't I might get less, or even a fine only. In the end I decided to compromise. I would say that I was going to go on increasing the volume of blood in my brain by legal means, such as standing on the head. In my interview with the probation officer I told him this. I said I didn't drink alcohol or smoke tobacco, because they were toxic. I had smoked hash because it is non-toxic, but in future I was going to use legal means to get high. In my opinion it was not the law's position to prevent me putting my own blood in my own brain by any means I chose. We had a friendly chat. The officer was obviously a lonely soul and this was his way of meeting people. He gave me a sweet.

The psychiatrist was a different kettle of fish. On the table in front of him was the open letter. He asked me about it and I told him he could read it if he wanted to know. Did I really believe this nonsense he asked. I said it was not a question of believing it. I knew from experience that it was correct. I asked him if he had ever smoked pot. He was a West Indian. He said he had tried it once but it had had no effect on him, though on other people it could produce psychotic reactions. He asked me if I had seen any other psychiatrists and I told him yes, Dr Dally at Westminster Hospital. He rang him. Dr Dally had been trying to contact me for his third degree questioning and now he found out why I was unable to attend.

The week dragged on. The highlight was when a friend showed me a tiny piece of hash he had got. We rolled a tiny joint with tobacco and smoked it. There was too little to make much difference, but it was nice to be able to beat the system. When the trial came up the probation officer made a little speech in my favour. The magistrate asked me if I intended to smoke hash in the future. I said no, but I would continue to increase my brainbloodvolume by legal means. I was given a year's conditional discharge.

I was free again. I walked out of court and took a deep breath of London air. Free I was, but my troubles were not yet ended. I still hadn't got that piece of bone out of my skull. I decided to leave it for a few months before trying again and let the hair grow. I was faced with this dilemma: officially I had trepanned myself. The news had spread. Should I now tell the true story or keep up the lie? I decided to keep up the lie for a few months, then complete the operation and no one would be any the wiser. What difference did a few months make? I wished I had never told the lie in the first place, but now I was stuck with it. It was easier to keep it up than tell the truth.

Amanda had been trying to fix it for Bart to be allowed to return. She had visited many officials, but it was no use. Though I found her very attractive, I considered her Bart's girl, so did not make a pass at her. However, after a few months and endless games of Go, when all her efforts had come to naught and we were enjoying each other's company, it seemed silly to hold off any longer and, with the understanding that Amanda and Bart would continue their relationship, we came together. Bart, who was homeless and without money, was back with his wife in Amsterdam and here were we in London. Life became fun again. Love was in the air. Amanda was highly intelligent. Being the youngest of four children, with a brother and two sisters above her, she had become an expert psychologist through observing their behaviour and learning from their mistakes and later became my guru of the Unconscious. Above all she was very much herself, with her own views arrived at on the basis of her own experience.

At this time I was doing the book-keeping for Michael Rainey's shop for £10 a week. I only had to go in a few times a week and balance the accounts, so it suited me well. I preserved my freedom at the same time as getting an income. Michael had been in the position of having no money himself and he appreciated the difficulties. He showed himself to be a real friend. He was now on the crest of a wave; his picture was on the cover of *Life* magazine and his shop was patronised by all those who wanted to be thought "in" on the "Swinging London" scene. Soon he and Jane got married. Meanwhile Amanda and I were having a springtime romance in the London winter. As 1966 wore out and my hair grew again I began to think about doing the operation again.

In January of 1967 I decided to go ahead. I had thought of doing it in a different place, but in view of the fact that I was so close already I made up my mind to finish where I had left off. Again I took acid and sugar to be right on top of myself and this time everything went smoothly. By now I was something of an expert at injecting etc. I found the groove from the previous operation and got going. After some time there was an ominous sounding shlurp and the sound of bubbling. I drew the trepan out and the gurgling continued. It sounded like air bubbles running under the skull as they were pressed out. I looked at the trepan and there was the bit of bone in it. However, on closer inspection I saw that the disc of bone was much deeper on one side than the other. Obviously the trepan had not been in straight and had gone through at one point only, then the piece of bone had snapped off and come out. I was reluctant to start drilling again for fear of damaging the brain membranes with the deeper part while I was cutting through the rest, or of breaking off a splinter. If only I had had an electric drill it would have been so much simpler. Amanda was sure I was through. There seemed no other explanation of the shlurping noises. I decided to call it a day. At that time I thought that any hole would do, no matter what size. I bandaged up my head and cleared away the mess. As I was high anyway I didn't expect to notice any difference that day.

The next morning, when I woke, I felt fine but I couldn't really judge whether it had made a difference. It was a month or two before the wound had healed sufficiently for me to be able to feel with my fingers. I could feel a deep crater, with the deepest part at the bottom on one side. It was impossible to feel whether there was a hole or not. This created a doubt in my mind. Was there no end to this bloody business? It wasn't for the high that I wanted a hole in my head; I could get much higher in other ways anyway. It was more of an insurance policy, to ensure that I retained a youthful brain metabolism for life, a platform from which I could continue to make exploration trips into the universe of expanded consciousness. But I did want to be sure that I had got that and the evidence was inconclusive. What a drag, just like gravity!

Soon after this third attempt Amanda and I started reading Freud. Both of us drank thirstily at the fountain of his insight for more than a year, consuming his books at the highest level with large amounts of sugar to maintain the necessary concentration. It was an unforgettable experience. To me it was more of a revelation than to Amanda. Intuitively she had known many of the facts before, without having been able to express them. I was knocked out by it all. A new dimension to life appeared, the Unconscious. Freud's humour and his intensely meaningful prose (translated into English of course) were both beautiful and rewarding. We started analysing our dreams after reading *The Interpretation of Dreams*, surely one of the greatest books, if not the greatest, of the twentieth century, and I found this scientific method of self-analysis infinitely superior to the poetic gropings I had been attempting before. It was a disturbing period. I began to think I must be the most neurotic person in the world, since I could identify with almost every word. I had constructed a self-image which kept crumbling to pieces as one layer of illusion after another was peeled away to reveal a yet more infantile reality beneath it. At the end of the day I would think at last I'd reached the bottom of this well. I wanted to reach firm ground, to be able to say well this is how I am, for better or worse, but the further I went the more I discovered and the farther off the end appeared. After fourteen long books and copious note-taking I began to feel I was getting the hang of Freud. It would be quite impossible to master all the details without devoting many more years to the subject, but the general ideas I had grasped and I found them undeniably true. Spotting the latent motives beneath the apparent reasons for people's behaviour could also be incredibly funny.

One day, on a railway station, I saw a book by Wilhelm Reich on the news stand. I knew he had been one of Freud's most brilliant disciples, so I bought the book. It was called *The Function of the Orgasm*. It was a great book and led me to buy another of his, called *Character Analysis*, which was equally good. Reich's work came just at the right moment to cap the mountain of Freud. It was just what I had been looking for, an explanation of the way repression manifests itself in physical terms. I completely understood Reich's explanation of the neurotic character armour which the individual builds up to protect himself against reality. His "muscular vegetotherapy", not all that different to yoga exercises, was another aid to self-discovery. With the knowledge gleaned from these two authors I felt that I was now equipped for the long haul towards full self-realisation. I had got right under the façade with which I kept the world at bay and was on the road. The only obstacle in my way was the doubt about my operation. I had convinced myself that I had got through to begin with, but the evidence of feeling the hole had been so inconclusive that I had started to suffer increasingly from doubt. I could see so clearly that it could all have been wishful thinking. Of course I had wanted the original lie to be erased and forgotten and of course I had wanted to get the whole performance over and done with. Supposing I had got through but the hole wasn't big enough – how typical of me, I thought, to have a hole just that size that you couldn't tell if it was a hole at all. Still enveloped in Freud's world, I saw it would be just my neurotic style to be pretending to be what I wasn't, the younger brother trying to do what the older one did, putting on a big act. One thought kept recurring: if I had got a hole in my skull I was sure I wouldn't have this uncertainty. I began thinking of doing it again. Was I completely hung up on drilling holes in my head? No, but I couldn't go on living in doubt. I had told everyone that I had a hole in my skull. I had to know the truth myself. All this took time to crystallise in my mind. Meanwhile there was the future to think of and the problem of making a living.

In the winter of '67-'68 we had been to Amsterdam to stay with Bart and Barbara for three months before being asked to leave by the Dutch authorities because our visas had expired. Before we left we asked Bart to teach us the art of colouring prints, so that we could do that for money. In a week he had taught us all there is to know and we had had time to start practising on some old prints. Back in London we were now doing this, colouring enough prints per week to pay for all we needed. Neither of us fancied the idea of colouring prints for a lifetime however and, since there was no prospect of making a living teaching the mechanism at present, we began to think of a way to make a lot of money in a short time. There is no way that I know of in fact, so we decided to start with what we had got and expand from there. We had the knowledge of how to colour prints and the watercolours and paintbrushes and enough money to buy some prints of our own and colour them. This we decided to do. Our first purchase was of ninety prints for £23. Having coloured and mounted them we set off to sell them. Where should we go? What about department stores? We looked in the Yellow Pages. The first one listed was the Army and Navy Stores in Victoria. We went there and asked if they had a picture department. Yes, on the third floor. As we stepped out of the lift we met a woman and asked her where the picture department was. By chance she happened to be the picture buyer, Mrs Grant. She looked at our mounted prints of London scenes from Harrison's History of London, nice eighteenth century copper engravings, and bought twenty six at £3 each, a total of £78. We were in business. When we left the building and were safely in the street we looked at each other and roared with laughter. It was so easy!

We decided to become millionaires as soon as possible. It wasn't easy to predict a rate of growth with accuracy, so we thought we'd better give it a decade. Both of us agreed that we'd rather spend ten years' concentrated money-making and then be rich than have the money problem with us for the rest of our lives. It was also an enjoyable game to play together at the highest level, hatching a plan, carrying it out and seeing it succeed. We kept high all the time.

By 1969 we were beginning to make some money and in the summer we drove to Morocco. There we rented a house on the sea for two months. When we got back to the Embankment, Amanda was painting a window when she saw a pigeon on the window ledge looking very sick. It kept stumbling and falling over. Within an hour it had died. As I climbed out to pick it up I noticed a little ball of fluff quivering under the arch made by a buttress of the house. It was a baby which couldn't have been more than a week old. It had no feathers, only some furry down with a few spikes sticking through it. Amanda had the excellent idea of using a paintbrush to feed it with. She mixed some Weetabix and milk in a saucer and then scooped some up on the bristles and offered it to the little birdy. At first he needed some persuading, but he soon got the hang of it. Quickly he grew as he demanded more and more food with his shrill, insistent squeaking. You'd have thought the world was going to end if he didn't get some more at once. In a few weeks he had become a gawky fledgling. He hadn't any pigeon parents to imitate, so it was interesting to see how his instincts carried him through. Flying he learnt by trial and error, attempting vertical take-off. He flapped his wings frantically until he just hovered above the ground in extended jumps. We took him to the country to see if he would find it easier in the wide open spaces. We stayed with Amanda's parents, who had remained our loyal friends and supporters all through this time. As the four of us went for a walk through the fields, Birdy followed us, also walking. He thought he was one of us. It was very funny watching him run through the long grass trying to keep up. Soon he could fly beautifully, swooping and gliding in great show-off circuits over our heads before coming in to land on a shoulder. His voice broke, his eyes went orange and Birdy was grown up. Somewhere we read that pigeons can live up to thirty five years. Birdy showed no signs of leaving home. The window was always open, but he rarely used it. He was fixated on Amanda. He followed her around and nestled on her shoulder, cooing sweet nothings in her ear. Nothing looked like changing the pattern and it never did. What was most noticeable about his completely unrepressed behaviour was the large part motivated by the wish to have the undivided attention of his loved one.

Amanda had always wanted to go to America. I too wanted to go back, but I could wait. As the print business was going quite well, Amanda decided to go to New York in the spring of 1970. She could sell some prints to pay for the trip. This seemed an ideal opportunity to finally put paid to my doubts about the hole. I wanted to be alone to do it. It was my problem and I would solve it alone.

I remained in the flat with Birdy for company. When Amanda was away Birdy was much nicer to me. I was no longer the rival. He cuddled up to me. After two or three days he had adjusted to the new situation and we were getting along fine. He would make his nest in my chair and only got cross if I got up for any reason. One evening, however, he suddenly got up himself and walked over to the telephone and started pecking it. This was not something he had ever done before. I was reading a book and the pecking slightly got on my nerves. After a minute or two the phone rang and, lo and behold, it was Amanda from New York. She had a few words with Birdy. Was it telepathy? I would say so.

After Amanda had left I got all the equipment together. This time I would make absolutely no mistake. I was so familiar with the routine by now that I could almost do it blindfold. I decided not to take any drugs this time and went to work. I was using an electric drill and I had decided to do it just above the hairline in the middle of the forehead. I had been drilling for about half an hour when suddenly there was a burn-out in the cable connecting the drill-head to the motor. This really made me laugh. You won't beat me this time you old fox, Gravity, I thought. I put a bandage round my head and took the drill downstairs to Mr Lea, who lived in the basement and was an expert at carpentry and engineering. Mr Lea inspected the damage and said he could fix it. In an hour or so he had mended it. I thanked him warmly. It was getting late, so I decided to wait until the next day to complete the job. I had to clear the room up and resterilise all the instruments and so on.

The next day I resumed work. It was not long before I was through. This time I was not in any doubt. The drill-head went at least an inch deep through the hole. A great gush of blood followed my withdrawal of the drill. In the mirror I could see the blood in the hole rising and falling with the pulsation of the brain. I was elated. I had conquered fear and now I had conquered doubt. I waited to see if I noticed a change. Over the next three or four hours I got gradually higher; actually the feeling I had was one of increasing lightness, literally as if a weight was being lifted from my mind. I began to notice it probably an hour after I'd finished the operation, and then it grew stronger. I hadn't really known what to expect and it was rather exhilarating feeling this gradual lightening. Would it last? Well it lasted until I went to sleep, and the next morning I was amazed to find that the feeling of lightness was still there. I hadn't come down. And in the days that followed I realised that it was a permanent change in my consciousness that had taken place. I was in a better place, ready for anything.

What conclusion was I to draw about the last time? I could not be sure it had not made some difference, but it certainly wasn't the whole difference. I'm inclined to think that the hole was too small, nothing more than a slight crack, which wouldn't have been sufficient to do the trick and would anyhow have sealed again, whereas a proper hole would not seal. The skull has a different origin from the other bones in the skeleton and holes in it do not seal, though the edges do round off after a time. This hole was about seven millimetres in diameter. It was definitely enough. I felt that this was the optimal level of brain metabolism (ie without the need for extra sugar). The hole was big enough to allow the full beat to express itself in the brain arteries. I regretted having publicly stated, both in writing and talking, that I had succeeded before. On the other hand I was proud of having had the courage to admit the doubt and take the necessary steps to put things right.

When Amanda came back from New York she noticed the difference in me at once. It finally convinced her that the sooner she solved her own problem the better it would be. Before that she had not been in a hurry, but now she really saw the advantage. She decided to do it herself and make a film of it for propaganda purposes. She bought a super-8 movie camera, which she later used mainly for filming her beloved Birdy. Amanda is a very thorough person. She wants everything to be just right before she does anything, so she set about preparing everything, including herself. She had seen the hash I made of my early attempts and she was determined not to make the same mistakes. She was familiar with the procedure and she wanted to do it herself so that she would be in complete control throughout.

Gradually over six months she prepared herself. When the day came she got the room ready. She laid out all the instruments on a table covered with a white sheet. She wore a simple long white dress with a bathcap plastered down over her hair to prevent any getting in the wound and infecting it, and she set up the camera for me to film the proceedings. All this activity as director was a help; having to focus on the filming made the actual operation almost incidental. Once it was all set up she set to work in front of a full length mirror. There was a white sheet on the floor as well. I remember the beauty of the first drops of dark red blood falling on it, like red tulips on a carpet of snow (a sight I once saw after a freak snowstorm in May).

After she had completed the job she put on an antique kaftan we had bought in Morocco, richly coloured in green, gold and red with a turban of silver, blue and gold over the bandage. She looked exceptionally beautiful and radiant as we went out to a party we had been asked to.

Now that we were both trepanned, we set about campaigning together. Amanda edited the film, cutting in shots of Birdy flying over the topiary at Beckley and pecking about on the window ledge etc, and I made a soundtrack to accompany it, with pieces of a Mozart string quartet, Thelonious Monk, Fats Waller and others – Sonny Rollins's rasping sax during the drilling – and Amanda gave a quiet commentary explaining the reason behind it. We called the film *Heartbeat in the Brain*. It was no more than 20 minutes long. We showed it first at the ICA in the Mall and subsequently gave showings in many places, including New York and Los Angeles. In New York Amanda put on an exhibition at PS1, an avant garde gallery space in Queens. She called it "Trepanation for the National Health". Hundreds of people came to see it. It was quite spectacular. Amanda blew up stills from the film, some as big as 30 by 40 inches, some half that size, and we made a frieze all around this enormous room, 30 feet by 40 feet. The frieze had three layers, one above the other and was uninterrupted all around the room, completely covering the walls. It was an extraordinary sight, positively Egyptian in scale, these vast colour photos of someone drilling a hole in their head with pieces of text superimposed in places giving the explanation.

Later Amanda stood for parliament on the platform "Trepanation for the National Health". As the election agent I had to get ten citizens to endorse the candidate. I knocked on doors and explained that the aim was to have trepanation available on the NHS for anyone who wanted it done. The standard British sang-froid allowed people to keep a straight face as they listened to my pitch and eventually I got the required signatures. We had to make a deposit of £150, which we would lose if we didn't get a certain rather large number of votes, and we were in the race. We got a fair amount of press exposure, photos of Amanda with Birdy and then, after our first son, Rock, was born, others with him; I remember one caption, "Baby Rock with Hole in Head Mother". When the count was announced on the balcony of Kensington Town Hall, we got 49 votes. Four years later Amanda ran again and picked up 137.

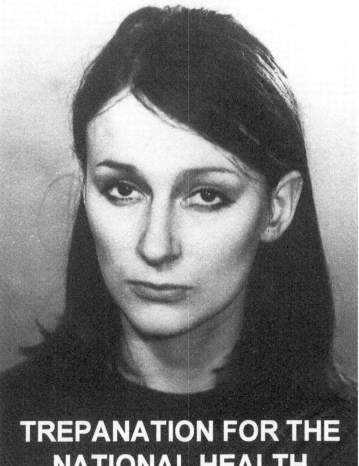

POSTSCRIPT

All of this took place nearly forty years ago. In the intervening years Amanda and I lived together for twenty eight of them, had two boys, Rock and Cosmo, who are now grown up and successful in their chosen careers; Rocky is in politics and Cos is a documentary filmmaker. Eventually we separated, but we are still good friends. In a sense we grew up together, sharing so much and insulating each other against the isolation which comes with avant-garde knowledge. It was the centrepiece of my life and Amanda was my other half, a lover and companion, a wonderful mother for our children and just the best friend a man could have to live with.

Some time in 1994, while Amanda and I were living separately, me in the Embankment flat in London and she at Beckley, I booked two tickets to a play at the National for us both. At the last moment Amanda rang to say that something had come up and she couldn't come. "Why don't you ask Jane?" she said. I rang Jane, but she couldn't come. "Why don't you ring Rose?" she said. Rose was her daughter. I rang Rose, but she said she was going to dinner with Michael, so she couldn't come either. "Jenny, my flatmate, might like to go, though", she said. "Jen, do you want to see a play at the National?" she called. Yes, came the reply. She put Jen on the phone. We arranged to meet in the foyer. "How will I recognise you?" I asked. "I'll be wearing green velvet trousers and a purple velvet coat", she said. "That shouldn't be too difficult", I said. Sure enough, I spotted her at once. She was outstanding, tall and beautiful. But hold it, I told myself – she's not for you. She was of a completely different generation. She could have no interest in me.

But wishes persist, regardless of the rational mind, and a month or two after that I was alone at Beckley and Mark Palmer, an old friend and neighbour – and incidentally an old Trojan of the sixties, who had taken to the life of a gypsy, living in a horse-drawn caravan and trading at Appleby Fair in ponies that he bred – rang me up one day and said there was going to be a rave in a barn. Why didn't I come? I loved raves, the ecstatic dancing in the loved-up crowd, so I thought why not, and why not ask Jen to come? So I did, and she said yes. Wow!

In fact she turned up with a man – oh well. Actually it turned out that he was an old boyfriend taken for protection, but I wasn't to know that. Anyway the rave was fun and they stayed the night and then left the next day. Jen sent me a thank-you postcard, saying "Dearest Joey..." – the postcard was a Vermeer painting with a lute in it; she couldn't have known that I played the lute. Was that an omen?

Later that year I was staying with Jane in Shropshire for a party and Jen was at the party. As a crowd of people squeezed between two rooms in a narrow doorway we passed each other. Jen, with her back against the doorpost, touched lips with me as I passed. That was it. I knew now that my wildest dream could come true. Our romance had begun.

Jen was fascinated by the hole in the head. She didn't know if it was something real or if I was in fact just a nutcase. She wanted to find out for herself. After she had known me for several weeks she asked me if I would trepan her. I said no. I didn't want to take advantage of the situation. Undeterred, Jen went to an old friend, Dave, and asked him if he would do it for her. Dave was the son of a brain surgeon as it happened, not that he had any such training. But he was something of a DIY expert. He could take a motorbike to bits and put it together again. Amazingly, he agreed to perform the operation for Jen. I said I would teach him everything necessary. On the day it all went smoothly. I remember Jen bounding down the stairs with a bandage round her head after it was over. She was in a joyful mood. Later she wrote an article about it, which was printed in *The Independent on Sunday* (see p. 185).

Jen got pregnant. We had heard about giving birth in water and we found that the Chelsea and Westminster Hospital had three birthing pools in their nativity department. The birth was a wondrous occasion. We knew it was going to be another boy and we had already named him Rudy Blu. Jen took no pain-killers or any artificial aids. Towards the end of the contractions we went to the pool room. I was told to get into the pool to control the temperature of the water to that of the body. Since it was an enormous pool that could have held ten people comfortably this was no easy matter. I was supposed to make alterations by turning on or off the hot or cold tap. I was amazed that in this flagship National Health Service hospital with all the latest equipment etc there was not a thermostat that controlled the temperature automatically. However, apart from this, which I didn't mind in the least, since it kept me busy (perhaps this was the point!), everything was as perfect and convenient as could be. When Jen got into the pool the relief was immediate and made the final contractions much easier. When Rudy emerged he didn't take his first breath until the midwife brought him up out of the water and placed him in my arms. A bonus was that he was clean, not covered in the slimy amniotic fluid. Altogether it was a perfect birth. It went without a hitch and was all the more memorable for me for being actively involved in it, if only in the most peripheral way. It was nine months to the day from Jen's trepanation. The usual adoration set in.

Jen and I got married. Jen's maiden name was Gathorne-Hardy (her father, Jonny, is a well-known writer) and she was glad to change it for something shorter. We have lived happily together now for twenty years. Rudy has grown up and is a singer/songwriter in a band. Two years ago we had a daughter, Lily. Life is good.

Bart died three years ago. Amanda and I are still trying to pass on his message to (it must be said) a pretty disinterested world. Amanda has since then set out to provide the scientific proof of Bart's discoveries. To this end she set up the Beckley Foundation, with a twofold aim, to instigate scientific research into psychedelics and the phenomenon of expanded consciousness and to reform global drug policy. In both spheres she has had outstanding success; the Beckley Foundation Scientific Advisory Board was established with leading international scientists, including Albert Hofmann, Alexander Shulgin, Colin Blakemore and David Nutt among others. When Nutt moved to Imperial College in London in 2009, together they set up the Beckley/Imperial Psychedelic Research Programme, which carries out pioneering research into psychedelic states of consciousness and their therapeutic use. She has also set up a collaborative programme with Professor Yuri Moskalenko in St Petersburg, studying the effects of trepanation on cerebral circulation, and this work has shown that trepanation increases the index of cranial compliance (which, as far as I know, is another way of saying arterial pulsation), the decrease of which is associated with cognitive decline. It is now being investigated as a preventive measure against Alzheimer's disease, as was reported in an article in the *New Scientist* in June 2009.

After years of struggle to get taken seriously by the "adult world", she has now attained a position of great influence and, in the small but growing "psychedelic world", the Beckley Foundation is established as the leading light in both the scientific and political spheres. Their Public Letter in 2011, headed "The Global War on Drugs has Failed: It is Time for a New Approach", was signed by seven ex-presidents, including Jimmy Carter, two existing presidents, of Colombia and Guatemala, one ex US secretary of state, George Schultz, eleven Nobel prize winners, scientists, writers, an archbishop, Desmond Tutu, and many other international luminaries, artists, musicians, entrepreneurs (Richard Branson) et al.

Her energy is unflagging, her patience unending, her sense of humour undiminished, together with her instinct for the "bon mot". I will give two examples: when someone once asked her what she thought of Giscard D'Estaing, the French president, she replied, "I think he looks very d'estainguished!". I also remember her saying, after forgetting something, "I always forget that I've got no memory." With her husband, Jamie Wemyss, she floats around her beloved Beckley under a large canvas sun hat that we bought in Venice Beach in 1979, picking flowers for the vases that adorn the hall until interrupted by the endless telephone calls that demand her attention.

I think it worthwhile now to add to the foregoing story two pieces, one a brief account of Bart's life, particularly as it related to mine, and secondly a conclusion in which I make as objective an evaluation of the benefits of trepanation to me personally as I can.

BART
(TOO CLOSE TO THE SUN)

Towards the end of the summer of 2004 I had a phone call from Arie, a friend from Amsterdam, to tell me that Bart had died. It was a shock. He had died in hospital. It was a merciful release from a purgatory, which, it must be said, was mainly of his own making.

Well, he was gone. Bart was dead. It was a sad day, a sad ending to an amazing life, an amazing man, a true genius. The word "genius" is so debased today that a new one is needed for a man of his stature. His genius was of a different magnitude to that of a pop singer or a hat designer. He was a genius of science, a thinker of the highest rank, whose insight brought to light hitherto hidden mechanisms of the mind. There was a flip side to his genius however. He was unable to compromise. It was all or nothing with him. No doubt that was part of the package.

He was an extremely rare human being, blessed with a clear vision and an encyclopaedic knowledge of biology and medicine. He never forgot anything he had learned. His mind was organised like the best run library, facts filed away in the most logical order, available when he needed them to reinforce his extraordinary insight. He simply saw the way the brain worked. No one before him had ever seen it so clearly. He had an overview, he saw with the acuity of an eagle from way above the wood, then was able to go into the wood and see the way the trees were planted. It was all a matter of the way the blood was distributed, how repression was used in this process and how the word was the instrument with which the self effected this distribution.

The key discovery was that the way man exercises his free will is by controlling the distribution of blood in the brain. Animals act essentially by reflex, their basic reflexes being modified by the conditioning of custom and the immediate dangers of local circumstance. They do not have the ability to rehearse actions in their minds and make decisions on the basis of comparison of one possible course with another. This is what we mean by free will. Blood distribution in the brain is effected through the agency of the Ego, which puts the speech system in control; it has associations with all the centres of higher function in the brain, excluding, that is, the most basic reflex actions which are beyond the reach of consciousness.

That blood is distributed to the centres in action is beyond question. What no one had explained before is how the individual exercises control over it. Bart saw that it was through the use of the word. In animals the blood goes where the action is. Any part of the brain stimulated by a sensory perception attracts blood to it. Animals act by reflex. A stimulus is received in the brain and a reflex reaction occurs. These reflexes can be inhibited by events, so that, for example the smell, sound or sight of a cat may stop the mouse from going straight for the cheese. But the extent to which this happens is severely limited; it does not go beyond the immediate circumstances of the action. With man, on the contrary, the number of actions which take place on pure reflex are severely restricted. There are certain fields in which reflex action predominates, such as sport or battle, but even then they are circumscribed by rules and include a great many rehearsed or conditioned reflex acts. What Bart saw was the connection between the word and the distribution of blood. He realised that the speech system was linked to the arterial system in the brain, with the recognition of the word's meaning being the conditioned stimulus which kept the chain of associated words, or thought, moving like a caterpillar round the twin hubs of the talking and listening centres. Recognition in the listening centre was the stimulus for the injection of more blood into the talking centre for the articulation of the next word. All the organs involved in these two functions, recognizing and articulating, were coordinated (by being supplied with blood) under the control of this mechanism, which he called the Ego. Bart supplied what was missing in Freud, the physiology of concentration and repression. Freud had attempted to provide it in his "Project for a Scientific Psychology", but had abandoned the attempt in the end. He had seen it as the distribution of nervous energy or electricity, the charge, or cathexis as he called it, of images.

In Freudian terms the Ego gives the meaning of the word the individual assigns to it, while the Super Ego is the meaning given by the individual's parents or "higher authorities". The Id is the world of instinct, reflex action. Man thus, with this conditioned reflex mechanism, constructs a representation of the outside world in his imagination, his inner world. If an image (to be exact, the word representing it) is placed under a taboo it is repressed and blocked from function. It does not appear on the screen of consciousness. In other words man has the power to direct the blood where he wills, through the agency of the speech system, which itself is ensured priority in blood supply by means of the Ego's grip on the brain's arteries, which denies blood to other parts for this purpose. All of this Bart saw with intellectual insight, a feat of imagination I can only wonder at. I remember him explaining it to me for the first time. We were in an apartment in Ibiza and the window was open. On the balcony were some plants in pots. As he was telling me how the blood could be directed to a particular part of the brain with pinpoint accuracy, I "saw" a shower of rain fall as if from a sprinkler onto one particular plant among the others. The sky was pure blue. I was spellbound by his description and had conjured up this vision in my imagination and projected it onto the real world outside.

The crucial thing here is that man does not, like other animals, depend on outside stimuli alone for action in the brain but can create his own action by conducting manoeuvres around his imagination with the use of words. The original impetus for a line of thought may come from an external stimulus but, once started, the train is self-propelled.

So what exactly is so crucial about this discovery? Why is it so important? This is the question that echoes round my brain every time I say that it is so important. If it is so important, why do I seem to be among so very, very few people who agree with me? Why can't everybody see it? What "it" am I talking about?

Then, when I start thinking how to explain it, I decide that I'll have to start right at the beginning again. You see it's about the human condition, about the mechanics of the mind. The impulse to enquire into our nature, to understand how we come to be what we are and the motives for our behaviour, is behind the evolution of culture and civilisation. As Descartes said, "cogito ergo sum". There has been no real advance on that since then. There's the thinking animal said Descartes, this is what's going on in his head said Bart.

Not only did Bart see how the speech system controlled the blood distribution in the brain but also he saw how the level of brain metabolism depended on the volume of blood available to the brain cells and how this could be increased, leading to a transcendental or mystical experience. He realised that this elevated state of mind, so highly valued throughout history, could be reached by everybody. By defining the way this experience took place he was not taking the mystery out of the experience, just out of the description. In thinking about this Bart realised that the upright position had affected the economy of blood volume in the brain, resulting in a "fall" which had always been given mythical significance but could now be scientifically explained. It could also be remedied.

These different levels of brain metabolism, or consciousness, enabled the individual to attain the highest overview and deepest insight which his intelligence rendered him capable of. The risks of taking drugs to reach these higher levels were also something which knowledge of the mechanisms involved could eliminate. This knowledge represents a great step forward for man, enabling him to enjoy the visions of the enlightened without risking his sanity and health, as Prometheus did for instance.

Man is not only a thinking animal, but also a drug-taking one. Ever since he could he has been taking something to get high. This is a fact we can't escape even if we should want to, which experience shows a considerable number of people do. Why do these killjoys feel so strongly about it? There is no question that something about it threatens something in their minds. After all it is something that happens exclusively in the drug-taker's mind, the high, so why should it be a threat to anyone else? It's the behaviour it leads to that is the threat, they will say. Well, the behaviour, if it is anti-social in some criminal way, may lead to the courts.

That's what they are there for. But why should merely the taking of something to put more of your own blood into your own brain be a punishable offence? The threat, they will say, is something more insidious. What, I think, they're afraid of is the subversive effect of expanded consciousness, the undermining of blindly accepted values, social conventions, religious beliefs. It makes everybody look again at everything they have accepted without thinking before. As Bob Marley put it, "when you smoke the herb it reveals you to yourself". It is my faith that this is a good thing and that, if taken with knowledge of the safety measures, mind-expanding drugs have a beneficial effect on the development of a healthy, sane and socially responsible individual.

There are two aspects of religion, the Word and the Love of God. The Word is what the followers of religions use to pursue their aim of converting everyone to their faith. It is an explanation of existence and life after death. It becomes a law that must be obeyed and enforced on pain of torture and death. The Love of God is an experience, an elevated point of view from which all arguments seem absurd. It was Bart's fate to be the one who first illuminated this duality. The tyranny of the Ego in the adult's brain, his confinement to the world of words, of reason and unfeeling logic, can be lifted by a trip to the upper regions where the spirit is free to express itself unfettered by the restrictions, prejudices and taboos that normally inhibit it. This is the realm of love, where we all long to live, where we feel united with each other and all other creatures, with the whole of existence of which we feel a part. That, in my opinion, is an experience of the very highest value and should not be withheld from people but, on the contrary, strongly encouraged.

So, to return to my point, whereas science provides us with a replacement for the Word of God in explaining existence in general, taking psychedelic substances gives us direct experience of the Love of God. So what I am saying is that empiricism has replaced revelation as the source of knowledge in the physical, biological and chemical worlds, and taking psychedelics provides the spiritual complement to this logical sphere.

Bart was a giant in a world of pygmies. He knew that what he had discovered was the truth and the tragedy was that in the end he realised it was never going to be accepted by his peers. He died alone and unknown, happy only in the satisfaction of knowing that he had discovered the scientific explanation of that most enduring of all religious myths, the Fall of Man. His contemporaries could huff and puff all they liked but his house was built of solid rock and will survive long after they are all forgotten. As Schopenhauer said, truth goes through three stages: first it is ridiculed, then it is violently opposed and finally it is accepted as self-evident – well, what's so extraordinary about that, it's common sense; come on, we've always known that!

If we saw ourselves as apes who have cleverly shaped the noises we make into recognisable words (soundbites) rather than beings apart from and above the animal kingdom, we would have a more realistic view of our situation. Bart realised that the assumption of the upright position had put the maintenance of our sanity in jeopardy. Our survival depends on thinking, which depends on speech, which depends on there being enough blood in the speech centres. He realised also that the urge to get high was a result of this adaptation, to restore the blood lost to gravity when the skull sealed at the end of growth. This indeed is the religious impulse, the wish to feel at one with the whole of existence, to transcend the dualistic world of the Ego and experience the divine sense of unity, the love and peace that "passeth all understanding". When he was given LSD as a medical student he had that experience. He realised that paradise was in the brain, not beyond the grave. However, if heaven was in the brain, so was hell, the descent into meaninglessness, madness, loss of self-control. He made it his business to look into the phenomenon of "expanded consciousness" and find the material basis of it.

Vision, prophetic vision, great original insight, implies travelling to what Aldous Huxley called the "antipodes of the mind", to a viewpoint no one else has taken before. It is an isolated position, a tiny volcanic island in an ocean of unknowing which gradually expands until it links all the continents together and becomes the mainland.

What is the benefit of getting high? Oh my god, that is the question that's so hard to answer – why is it so important? Well, it's to make the most of what you've got – but that's just what you say I hear you saying, and let's face it, it's not exactly what most people would say, I've got to admit… because most people wouldn't call getting high important – they'd call it fun, or enjoyable or risky perhaps, but not important.

Well, to see its importance, you need to see the value of optimising the distribution of blood to all parts of the organism, not only the brain but the body too. It's a health measure. The thing to have faith in is your central nervous system. It can perform miracles if you give it the blood. The arterial system is under the control of the central nervous system. Problems are caused by blockages in the system, arising from one cause or another, mental or physical, repression or bruising, infection, whatever. By understanding this the whole picture of health can be seen in a new light.

The point is that God is the high vision, looking down on all creation – it's a point of view that can be shared by everyone – you just have to go there. Here am I, talking about God, trying to explain to the world what was so important about Bart's discoveries. It's ironic, because Bart would never have talked about God, even thought about it. He was from a family of doctors, a scientist, a materialist, an atheist. But this is the point: it's the experience, not the word, that's important, as far as God is concerned; but it's the word, not the experience, that's important where the Ego is concerned. The trick is to transcend the Ego and get to God. Bart's work was defining both God and the Ego. Now do you see its importance?

To go back to the beginning, Bart was the first born son of a doctor, himself the son of a doctor. His mother was an upper class English woman. She died when Bart was one and a half, having just given birth to his younger brother. His father had supervised the birth. One can only imagine what a cataclysm that must have been for Bart and it must have been the determining factor in his future single-mindedness.

His father married again, a good and kind Dutch woman, not an intellectual at all. Bart was fond of her, but didn't identify with her. He transferred his Eros into the pastime of collecting reptiles and amphibians. That became the consuming interest in his childhood. In the holidays he would hitchhike across Europe and catch a variety of lizards and snakes, turtles, frogs, toads etc, which he brought back and kept in his bedroom. At one time he had over two hundred, including a crocodile, which used to sunbathe on the branch of a tree that he had fixed so that it stuck out of his window. He had caught it as a baby, but when he had grown to nearly full size much to the consternation of his neighbours, who eventually got up a petition to have it removed. He was forced to give it to the zoo, where he used to go and visit it regularly.

After puberty the lizards had to share his Eros with girls. He was extremely handsome and charismatic and his youth coincided with the explosion of liberality, not to say libertinism, that flowered in Amsterdam and made it the most progressive and avant garde city in Europe. He was friends with all the main figures in this movement, Jaspare Grootveld, Johnny the Self-Kicker, Simon Vinkenoog and others and took part in the "happenings" that filled the main square in the centre of the city, the first mass acid-taking events in the sixties, that prefigured Woodstock and the pop festivals that have become such mainstream fixtures in the youth calendar of today. As is so often, in fact normally, the case in life, the Dutch exhibit polar opposites in their national character, the strict, Calvinist Puritanism together with a reaction of extreme Epicureanism, which results in a hybrid of somewhat moralistic liberalism.

After leaving school and entering the University of Amsterdam to study medicine, another feature of Bart's life, that was to become significant much later, was his chosen method of making an income. In his spare time he became a tutor and was very successful in coaching students to pass exams. He advised his students to write out the information they wished to ingest at the same time as repeating it out loud. To avoid the problem of the material "going in one ear and out of the other" he recommended that they repeat the talking as often as necessary to ensure that it was thoroughly imprinted in their minds.

A story that he told about his early years reveals the way he thought. He had grown up from the cradle with the daughter of a doctor friend of his father. They played together and went to the same schools, from kindergarten through to high school. As infants they had promised to marry each other and for years after that Bart had had a guilty feeling because he no longer wanted to marry her. She was the first person who had told him of something "supernatural". She said that everybody had a guardian angel standing behind them. Bart asked her where exactly and she said "behind you". He turned his head round and said, " but I don't see anything." "That's because it turns round with you and is always behind you." "But I don't see anything behind you either." "That's because you don't believe it." "How can I believe it if I don't see it?" "I believe it and it protects me." "I prefer to protect myself, then I don't have to believe in anything I do not see," said Bart.

Sexually precocious, having slept with his first serious girlfriend at the age of fourteen – a relationship that lasted for four years – at the age of seventeen he took on the role of deflowerer for girls who had fallen in love with another boy but had denied their virginity. His father left him alone, having decided from the start to give him a free education. He accustomed his family to the fact that he was often busy with his lizards, snakes etc and on those occasions the door was locked. This made it easy for him to sleep with his girlfriend there. Her parents didn't object.

His room housed a giant terrarium, which he could walk around in. It had a jungle, a desert and a pond and the back wall consisted of concrete rock formations. The lighting and heating were adjustable, with an ultra-violet lamp which could be switched on occasionally to keep the animals on colour. He bred meal worms and white mice himself (for the snakes) and supplemented the diet with earth-worms, maggots, flies, cockroaches from the zoo and small fishes from an angling shop. He also had three rats that lived free in the room and their young provided further meals for the bigger animals.

One other story about his youth is worth telling and that is of the meeting with his guru of the esoteric, Henk. He met him while he was in a youth hostel in the Pyrenees on a lizard hunt. Henk was a psychology student from Amsterdam. He asked Bart all kinds of questions: what did he consider the most important thing? Himself. What was a genius? Someone who can always keep yes and no apart. What was man? A hairless talking ape. What was life about? The oxidation of glucose. He stayed on in the youth hostel until all his money was gone. Henk then took over and arranged everything. They travelled by train to Avignon on a platform ticket. Henk taught him how to deal with the conductor. Standing in the corridor, with the compartments behind them, when the conductor approached Henk went up to him, conversing seriously for a minute or two and thanked him profusely before slipping with Bart behind his back, so that he had passed them, and then stood still again. The conductor knew them by now and continued on his way unperturbed. In Avignon he asked a little old lady to get them a platform ticket and the deed was done.

Henk had studied hypnosis and he told Bart all the things he could make people do without their being aware of it. One night in the opera, before the performance had begun, Henk told him to point out anyone in the audience and he would make that person do whatever Bart wanted him to. Bart didn't believe him. He pointed to a man in a grey striped suit next to a lady in a purple dress. "What do you want him to do?" "Take his left shoe off, look in it and knock the heel." "Look for yourself and before you have counted thirty he will do it." Bart looked and counted and saw to his surprise that the man appeared to be bothered by something in his shoe and started to take it off. After that he saw ladies take shoes off and even undress themselves right there in the opera house and finally he was convinced that Henk could influence people from a distance. It was only later that Bart realised it was he himself who had been hypnotised.

He spent a lot of time with Henk, discussing the meaning of life, free will, chance, the spirit, God, life after death, telepathy, good and bad, beautiful and ugly, all kinds of subjects which he had never given so much thought to before. Henk gave him a list of writers to read, Plato, Nietzsche, Freud, Hölderlin, Rilke, de Lautréamont, then *The Epic of Gilgamesh*, *The Baghavad Gita* and *Upanishads*. Henk had systematically broken the law on nearly all points and had never been in trouble. Bart said that his contempt for other people was greater than he'd ever seen in anyone. He had justified his exclusive position with the determination that at the end of his travels he would offer humanity the "solution", and in case of failure would choose suicide on his thirtieth birthday rather than face a lifetime of humiliation.

Bart received a parcel containing a beautiful book of poetry and Henk's hand-written announcement of death with a black line around it and a farewell letter in very small handwriting. His body was found downstream from a spot where he had once left Bart in the Pyrenees when they had been walking together. He had disappeared for half an hour and then returned. A year later a friend of Bart's got a lift from a car in Sweden. In the back of the car he found a box with "old photographs" written on it in Swedish. He spoke Swedish and asked if he could look at the photographs. Among them he found a number of photographs of Henk. Apparently the Swede had been walking through the streets of Amsterdam a year before when Henk had approached him and asked him to take some photographs of him in different positions with a skull in his hands. Then Henk had asked him to develop them and print them and keep them for a year. Bart's friend explained to the Swede who Henk was and asked if he could keep the photos. The Swede agreed and the friend then gave them to Bart. By putting them in a certain order you could read all kinds of messages in them, but Bart said that with Henk he had never been certain of anything and the meaning had escaped him. Bart was eighteen at the time.

Bart's first experience with LSD had been in the course of his medical studies, as a volunteer in the company of two doctors and a psychologist. Five hours after taking it he had become very paranoid and had seen the psychologist as a devil with horns on his head, one of the doctors as a pig and the other as a chimpanzee. Finally he was given chlorpromazine to bring him down. He volunteered again and this time, after a couple of hours he got bored by the psychologists and said he wanted to go home. They gave him a chlorpromazine tablet, which he pretended to take but actually slipped into his pocket. After half an hour he said all the symptoms had disappeared and they let him go home. He then enjoyed the rest of the trip with his girlfriend Barbara, later to become his wife, going to a café and buying half a litre of gin to drink with her, then describing to her all his hallucinations on the white wall, first a circus, then Arabian belly dancers, then a sea battle during which the sea flooded out of the wall and he had to climb on a chair to save himself. After that he was so drunk that Barbara had to drag him into bed.

Among Barbara's friends he noticed several who, though around thirty years old, had the clarity of mind of seventeen-year-olds. On getting to know them he found that they all smoked marijuana. He had never wanted to go down that road, fearing that he would become addicted and end in prison. These friends all knew each other and together constituted a clan whose bad reputation was well known to him. He kept asking his new friends what the effect was and they kept saying "try it yourself and you will see." They said that by smoking he would become happier, but also unhappier, that he would enjoy life more and have more sadness. He read up about it and saw that all the researchers had found it to be non-toxic and non-addictive. Finally he decided to try it and was soon a confirmed smoker. He was surprised to find that no one knew what the action of the drug was. He got more and more interested in it. Typically one-track minded, he bored all his smoking friends with his obsessional questioning. Then at one party he saw Titi, a negro yogi, who stood on his head for quarter of an hour in the middle of the party, having first asked not to be left out when the joint was being passed around. When he questioned Titi about the action, Titi said, "I've smoked it for forty years, as much as I can get, and I've never experienced any harm, but often there isn't any or I have no money for it, so I stand on my head. That gets you just as high." That was the clue that put him on the right track, like Newton's apple. He suddenly saw that it must be more blood in the brain.

His friends and colleagues in the medical profession were unimpressed when he began to describe his ideas to them, telling them that consciousness could be expanded by increasing the volume of blood in the brain capillaries. They had never heard anything like that. This was in the late fifties. When he told them that you could get as high from standing on the head as from smoking marijuana it aroused no interest, rather suspicion of him. Offering them a joint didn't help. They refused it and he realised that it could get him into trouble. Gradually he was drawn more and more into the Bohemian set of drug-takers, artists, poets, musicians etc. When Barbara gave birth to their first daughter, they called her Maria Juana.

The time was coming for him to take his final exams. He set aside his studies of expanded consciousness to concentrate on the syllabus. He was confident that he had done the necessary work and had gained the required knowledge and experience. Bart had been asked by the professor of psychiatry to become his assistant when he had qualified. However, after his espousal of the cause of marijuana had attracted unfavourable attention in the higher echelons of the profession, he was one day summoned to the Rector Magnificus of the university to be told that he had been excluded from specialising in Amsterdam by that same professor. Shortly after that the professor of psycho-analysis telephoned him to say that he had been refused the necessary preliminary training to enable him to enter the circle of analysts. Since he was only working for a medical degree in order to specialise in those two subjects, he realised that it would be useless to stay in Amsterdam, so he sat for an American doctorate in the Hague. He passed in the top category, so that he could now practise in America after an internship of one year in a hospital. He still took the Dutch exam a bit later. He passed in all subjects except one, the oral part of Obstetrics, which he considered his best subject. He had to take the oral again and he found himself in front of the same female doctor for the second time. It was obvious to him that she was hostile and would never pass him. It may well have been the reputation he had acquired for his extra-mural activities. He had recently been busted for possession of marijuana. The police had raided his house and there had been a lot of publicity. As a result of that he had spent three weeks in prison. Sure enough she failed him again. This meant that he had to take the whole exam again three months later. But his grant had run out and the authorities refused his application for a further grant to live on for that period, on the grounds of "insufficient study results", so he had to postpone the exam until he could afford to prepare for it again.

His father had always said that he wished he hadn't practised medicine. He was vegetarian and recommended his patients a lot of physical measures, diet, exercises, cold baths in the morning, that sort of thing. When he retired he told Bart that, had he known what it would be like in advance, he would rather have studied Dutch and become a writer. He said that the most frustrating thing was that his patients didn't listen to his advice. It may well have been the memory of this that helped determine Bart's subsequent actions.

Meanwhile the most lucrative job he could get was assistant to a doctor in the country for a spell, to fill in for the doctor's partner, who was ill. In the evenings he continued his research and investigation into the mechanics of expanding consciousness and began writing his discoveries on a scroll. The scroll was about eight feet long and a foot wide. It read from top to bottom. Eight diagrams, each one illustrating a different method of pushing more blood up into the brain, were contained in egg-shaped spaces in the text which flowed around them. It was a work not only of great academic achievement, but also of aesthetic pleasure.

When he had completed the scroll he started distributing it among a few smoking friends whom he thought capable of understanding it. He also went to the leading brain physiologist to see if he could work out how to measure some part of the mechanism. He wanted to measure the effect of some of the seven other methods described first and keep the performance of trepanation by a surgeon until the end. The doctor was very doubtful that he would find any volunteers and was surprised when Bart handed him a list of twenty. He also hoped to be included himself in the course of the research. The only method of measurement that he could think of was to mark the csf with isotopes so as to track it being squeezed out, but this turned out to be impossible due to the toxicity of the isotopes. Neither he nor the doctor could think of another way. He gave up hope of being able to measure it and prove the mechanism indirectly. He considered the direct proof of standing on the head and observing the effect to be good enough, but the great physiologist was not about to do that. Anyhow he disagreed with Bart. He denied that trepanation suppressed the pulsation in the arteries. He had often measured it he said. Yes, said Bart, by sticking a hollow needle through the skull.

He went to see several surgeons and discussed the matter with them. Some of them said they knew exactly what he was talking about, but they wouldn't consider performing the operation for him. Disappointed, he finally gave up hope of any cooperation with the medical establishment. There seem to me to have been two influences at work here: on the one hand he was attracted to the Bohemian lifestyle, free sex, drugs etc, and on the other there was his father's disillusion with the practice of medicine. He had become something of a notorious figure in the small city of Amsterdam, where the intellectual community is like a village, everybody knowing everyone else's gossip. It would undoubtedly have been difficult for him to pursue his career there, since the doors had been slammed in his face. He would have had to go to

America, but he had no money, he had a wife and child and he was totally engrossed in completing his own work. He decided that he would have to perform the operation on himself.

He arranged to do it on a certain day and various friends said they would like to be present, one to film it, one to do a painting and another to write a report. It may be that these friends didn't really think he was serious and only realised that he was when he had gathered all the tools and materials together and was obviously about to start work. They got cold feet. They didn't want to be present in case anything bad happened. In fact at the last minute they stole all his tools etc and Simon Vinkenoog called the Public Health Service and asked a psychiatrist to come over. Bart was furious. His friends tried to mollify him, saying that, for humanity's sake, a great genius like him shouldn't be allowed to take risks with his very life. Simon rang Barbara, who was staying at a farm in the country and accused her of deserting her post. She told him not to act so crazily, Bart didn't want to commit suicide and knew exactly what he was doing.

The Public Health psychiatrist had several conversations with Barbara. He wanted to lock Bart up for treatment "for his own good". Barbara assured him that he was in full possession of his senses and not in need of admission to hospital. Bart decided to wait for a spell to let the hullabaloo die down and then do it later without telling any of his friends. Meanwhile he continued to distribute the scroll. He got a job in a factory to pay the rent and household expenses and with what was left over he got more scrolls printed by silkscreen in black and white, colouring the diagrams by hand. He sent them to magazines with permission to publish. From most of them he heard nothing or else got a note back saying they only dealt with "scientific matters". One or two said that it was interesting but could only be published after more research had been done into it. He found that most of the friends he had given one to had not had time to read it or weren't interested in scientific treatises or had given it to a doctor friend who had told them that what was written on it was not correct. Everybody had some criticism; if only he had written it differently, if only this, if only that. As news of the scroll spread in the smoking world, beatniks from all over the world started coming to visit him. His kitchen was empty of food as soon as he had stocked it up.

Around this time he met Onno, a brilliant young student of mathematics and physics, ten years his junior. He had been smoking weed since he was fourteen. He had been top of the class at school and no one had known that he took a quick puff between lessons. Later he had been busted for dealing and spent some months in prison. At his trial he had argued that hemp is non-addictive and had been placed on the opium law incorrectly. Even when his statement was confirmed by Dr de Vaal, a toxicologist of the highest repute, it did not result in his release. After prison he had met a different attitude from parents and teachers alike. He found it impossible to explain the facts to them. They wouldn't listen.

He went on smoking pot of course and then someone had given him peyote. He made up his mind that he was going to synthesise the active principle of the cactus, mescaline. With the help of a friend he had got so far that one day he visited Bart with a sticky black substance. Bart took some and found that it was indeed mescaline. They were extremely pleased and decided to make much more of it. Unfortunately a few days later his friend quietly left the city with all Onno's equipment and raw materials in his car. He was left with nothing.

Onno had not had LSD and Bart told him how overwhelming the experience could be. He couldn't get hold of any, so he decided to make it himself. He refined Hofmann's synthesis, making big savings in costs. Even so it required a lot of money. Bart got involved with an American friend, Fred, in a deal of three kilos of hash from Lebanon. Fred was looking for a chemist to teach him the LSD synthesis. Bart put Fred and Onno together and, with the proceeds of the deal, the project began. Further injections of cash were provided by Bart's ability to act as middle man and meeting place for travelling beatniks wanting either to buy or sell. Finally the process was completed. Then Fred took the wrong bottle to empty and wash out and most of it got lost. The three of them had so much fun with what was left that they decided to do it all over again. The chemicals were very expensive and it took ages to procure them, but eventually the synthesis was completed for the second time.

This was the first LSD in Europe produced outside the pharmaceutical companies' laboratories. Bart had the opportunity to test his deduction that hallucinations were a symptom of sugarlack. He now knew how to avoid the paranoia that can ruin a trip and found out that with an adequate blood sugar level he could function perfectly while top high.

Now that the LSD project was completed, he thought it was time to perform the operation. He did so behind closed doors, telling no one except Barbara. A week later he took part in a big happening in the Dam square in Amsterdam, at which it was arranged that the bandages would be taken off ceremonially by Robbie and Simon.

On top of the original bandage Bart had added thirty two metres of new bandages with HA HA HA HA painted on them in all sorts of colours. These were passed around the crowd.

He was surprised to find that there was not one mention of it in the press, so he decided to hold a press conference in a room in a hotel. On the evening before that took place he heard that several people didn't really believe that he had done it. As he had anyway wanted an x-ray of the hole, he decided to go to the department in the Wilhelmina Hospital, where he had taken dozens of x-rays as an assistant, and ask the surgeon on duty for a skull photo as proof for the press. He found it was the same woman doctor who had examined him in Surgery six months before (when he had passed) and she filled in an application for an x-ray photograph for him. He gave her a scroll in return. While he was waiting for the photos to be developed two psychiatrists, alerted by the surgeon, came in and asked him to answer some questions in a side room. One of them asked him: "Are you cured now?" He answered: "If I am cured, then you are sick. But I have never been ill. It's just that my brain functions are improved." A nurse came in to say that the photos were ready. One of the psychiatrists went off to examine them while the other stayed with Bart. The first one came back and reported to his colleague that yes, there was an irregularity in the forehead bone. They exchanged knowing looks with each other and then said, "Mr Huges, you'd better come along with us to the clinic". Bart explained that he was due to give a press conference at a hotel in five minutes' time. They checked with the hotel and found out that it was true. As Bart made to leave they jumped in front of the door and prevented him from going. They grabbed his arms and physically restrained him. Bart said that if they didn't let him go he would start proceedings against them. They said they couldn't possibly let him out of the hospital with an open connection between the brain and the outside world. Bart explained that there was no open passage to the brain, the skin had healed over a week ago. After an hour of banter, during which Bart told them that he would give them his description of the mechanism for them to read and then discuss it with them when they had done so, they finally let him go to the press conference on condition that he promised to return the following day.

After the conference he rang a lawyer and explained what had happened. He was assured that there were no grounds for detaining him if he returned the next day. In Holland an individual's freedom could not be taken just like that. Despite this assurance, when he did return the following day he was surrounded by ten white-coated male nurses and hustled into the high security department for seriously deranged patients, where he was kept behind locked doors for three weeks while the psychiatrists conducted all kinds of tests on him. Finally, after none of the tests showed him to be in the least mentally abnormal, he was released. To add insult to injury, a few weeks later he received a bill from the hospital!

Following his experiences of incarceration with the legal and medical professions, Bart decided to turn his back on the establishment and go his own way. Even in today's world, in which mind-expanding drugs have become so widely used, there is an almost unbridgeable gap between the "straight" and the "hip" worlds, but in the late fifties and early sixties the gap was more like outer space. To the "square" world talk of "expanded consciousness" was totally incomprehensible. They had no idea what Bart was talking about. With ignorance goes fear and the more he said to them the greater the threat they perceived. The taboo prevented them looking and listening with an open mind, while their aggression was fanned by the apparently anarchic behaviour of the youth in the streets, which was associated with drug-taking. Bart now concentrated on distributing the LSD and explaining to people about the safety measures, which is where I came in.

I have recounted how I met Bart and helped him with the description of his discoveries in English, how I took LSD with him and learnt about the safety measures, how we campaigned together in London during the sixties to try and get the message across, how he met Amanda and fell in love with her, then was barred from entering the country. What I must now relate is what happened thereafter to Bart.

When Amanda and I first started living together I knew of and respected her love for Bart. It was a somewhat awkward situation, but in the circumstances we decided to make the best of it. Bart was my teacher. I was definitely his disciple, though also a friend and companion in arms, as it were. Amanda was his lover, though in a certain sense his disciple too as she wanted to learn all about his discoveries and to learn how to live on the highest level, which indeed she did. The problem was that when all three of us were together, which we were for periods of time now and then, Bart couldn't treat Amanda as his lover, so he treated her as a disciple.

The turning point in Bart's life had been the death of his mother. He had obviously been the apple of her eye, the first born son. For the first two years of his life he had basked in the sunshine of her love. Her death, giving birth to a younger brother under the care of his father, must have aroused Oedipal feelings of a raging intensity in him. These feelings he successfully dealt with. The glow of confidence which those early years had engendered remained with him and the passion was sublimated into his work, in the first place particularly the collection and study of amphibians and reptiles, and later the study of the mechanics of the mind.

When I first met Bart, in Ibiza, in 1965 it was a time of great social upheaval. There was a feeling in our generation that we were the vanguard of a revolution in values, we were going to change the world, bring peace and common sense where madness and corruption prevailed. To a certain extent this is the usual thing for idealistic youth starting out in the adult world, but there was a special feeling at that time that we had tapped in to something universal with the psychedelic drugs. Here was the means of changing the values, opening everyone's eyes to the wider and higher reality. Tune In, Turn On, Drop Out.

Bart was a leader in this movement. He showed the way. However, whilst people wanted to know him, wanted to meet him, wanted to talk to him, they didn't listen to what he was saying.

What I mean by that is they would listen to the stories he told, and he could be very funny, but they wouldn't study his work. The fact is it is not everybody's cup of tea, the mechanism of brainbloodvolume. "Oh god, how boring" is the most frequent reaction to the sound of it.

Bart often discussed this problem with me. He told me he had decided to play Willy Nilly with it; first he would try Willy, letting everyone in and taking a chance on them picking up something. If that didn't work, he would then go into Nilly mode, not letting them in until they had studied his work. At the time I had no idea what he really meant by that, thinking it was just a manner of speaking.

When he came to London in 1966, that glorious year of Swinging London when England won the World Cup at Wembley and the Beatles conquered the world, it was the high point of the Willy period – there was even a World Cup Willy symbol! It was then that he met Amanda. This, I surmise, was the culmination of his unconscious dream, the finding of his lost mother. Amanda fitted the bill completely. She was a beautiful, aristocratic English girl. For a few months everything was coming up roses.

One day an official from the home office came to the Embankment and told Bart that his visitor's visa had expired. He must leave the country. When the official had left, Amanda said, his eyes filled with tears and he told her that it was all over. In that moment he must have foreseen the future.

After he was refused entry into the country when returning to London from Amsterdam, he stayed there with his wife Barbara and his daughter Juana. They had a small house in the Jordaan, the Bohemian quarter. In the winter of 1967 Amanda and I stayed there with them for several months. I worked with Bart on the English version of his autobiography, which he called *The Book with the Hole*, printed finally with a hole through the middle of the pages and cover. There it sat, a book with a hole through it. The hole had a diameter of perhaps two centimetres. It was a very good read. But now there began the Nilly period. Bart decided that he would only give the book to people who had studied his work.

There is no doubt that there was a megalomaniac strain in Bart's character. He was aware of his charisma. He knew he had a magnetic quality and he decided to use it as a weapon. If people wanted to know him it would have to be on his terms. They would have to do their homework first. He began to design a "Homework Sheet", a test which people would have to complete before meeting him. Gradually, over the years, this "homework" became his obsession. In this "sadistic" treatment of other people, compelling them to study his work on pain of exclusion from his company, there was also a fairly large component of masochism. It was a double-edged sword. If they couldn't see him, he couldn't see them. He was henceforward confined to the company of those who would willingly jump through all the hoops he erected for them, which limited his entourage to a rather small and subservient group. His old friends were excluded.

Bart needed people around him. A teacher needs pupils. In his mind he was also the world leader, leading the way to a promised land, and it was this "führer" fantasy which was now ripe for exploitation by the right person. He duly appeared in the form of Richard Hubner, a psychology professor from some German university. Richard had had a troubled childhood, having been hidden beneath the floorboards when the Nazis came to see his father. The sound of jackboots striding across the floor above his head had been traumatic and secretly had had the effect of causing him to identify with the oppressors and look out for an opportunity in life to get the upper hand, put his boots on and crack the whip. Meeting Bart at this juncture provided him with exactly the role he craved, the enforcer. A little "fascist" party was formed. With Bart's approval Richard was set loose to construct this brave new world.

The homework was institutionalised. Richard oversaw the development and implementation of the programme. The central plank of the dogma was based on Bart's teaching experience as a tutor in his student days, the oral repetition of the subject matter. Added to that was writing out Bart's description of his discoveries at the same time. The theory was that by doing this the pupil would be exercising all his speech faculties at the same time, reading, writing, speaking and listening. Repeating the exercise ten times would ensure that the information was well and truly imprinted in the mind. A final touch completed the picture. This should be done on hands and knees, or rather elbows and knees to be more precise, so that the head was held below the heart and gravity was on your side. In this position, so the songsheet went, the taboo was unable to prevent the truth passing the threshold of consciousness and enlightenment inevitably followed. So wasn't that a dainty dish!

You just had to do this and you were admitted to the Secret Society. It was quite hard work, because the homework got longer and longer. From being one sheet it became copying out the descriptions of both mechanisms, of brainbloodvolume and the Ego, as well as a comprehensive glossary of definitions of the terms used. To do it once would take at least an hour. It had to be done ten times. When someone wanted to join the group they would have to present the completed homework to Richard, who would then usher them in to Bart's presence. Their megalomanias complemented each other's. Richard got to be the "Oberbefehlshaber der Bewegung" (chief superintendent of the movement) he had always longed to be and Bart had the imaginary satisfaction of seeing the whole world bow down before him as they copied his work out.

Looking at the situation from a psychological point of view, it had replicated in an uncanny way the situation of Bart's childhood. My living with Amanda was rubbing salt in the wound. Yet again his mother had been removed by the younger brother. It was not hard for Richard to strengthen his position as right-hand man to the führer by casting us as the enemy within, an essential role in such organisations. Naturally neither Amanda nor I had learnt the mechanisms by the homework method. Soon the official line became that the ONLY way to learn it was by doing your homework. Anyone who taught it without having done the homework was a false teacher. Amanda, as his consort, was given a dispensation, but I was a false teacher. That was the very worst thing to be. To be ignorant was unfortunate, but to be a false teacher was criminal. False teachers had to be purged.

A number of people did do the homework and joined the group. A few trepanations were organised, some did it themselves and then helped others do it. As many as twenty people, perhaps more, came and went over the next few years. Every now and then a "conference" would be called of the faithful. Amanda and I tried to keep in touch with Bart. Amanda dutifully went over on visits to Amsterdam several times a year, but it became clear that although Bart wanted to marry Amanda, she first had to renounce me as a false teacher. This she was not prepared to do. She knew that I was as committed to spreading Bart's message as anyone, understood it completely and shared her view that the whole homework cult was basically a power game, which by its nature excluded more people than it attracted, moreover especially those people in positions of influence who might have been useful in bringing it to a wider audience. It was becoming a cult and wallowing in a sort of "early Christian" complex, exactly the wrong image in our opinion. It was a different world to that of two thousand years ago, when the word was passed from head to head, a world of mass media and instant trans-global communication. Bart wanted to ensure that his work was not forgotten. Both of us thought he was going the wrong way about it. Strong character though he was, he had a habit of investing the person he was closest to with infallibility and seeing no faults in them. Not only that, but he invested the whole world outside his coterie with the characteristics of an unfaithful lover. In his mind he was punishing the world for not listening to him, but the world wasn't listening and didn't give a fig. The complex grew and grew like an in-growing toenail. Gradually he became more and more exclusive. Even his family were excluded. He and Barbara had had another daughter, Talitha, but, as the game progressed and Barbara found herself treated like an untouchable because she hadn't done her homework, she couldn't tolerate it any more and left him.

All of this was grist to Richard's mill. Unfortunately he got carried away by the illusion of power. His behaviour became more and more erratic. He took a lot of speed. His appearance became more and more outlandish. He shaved his head. He was covered in pustular spots. He roamed the streets of Amsterdam like an escaped lunatic, shouting at people, daubing the walls with graffiti. He was arrested, locked up in the loony bin, then released. Eventually he set fire to a house he was squatting in. Finally he was found floating in a canal belly up.

Amanda and I had attended several of these conferences out of loyalty to Bart. At one point I had even done the homework so as to keep on the right side of him. It was a real drag to do it, but we thought it important to keep the door open, so that if at some time he changed his mind we would still be able to cooperate with him and help him present a more human face to the world. An edict had been issued that only those who had done the homework could attend the conference. Although we would much rather not have attended the conference and been subjected to the usual boring discussion on how to get people to do the homework, we decided it was best if I overcame our resistance and did the damned thing for his sake. It did enable us to keep in communication.

On occasions Bart came and stayed with us, once in Morocco, where we had a nice time catching lizards and toads, two of which we took back to the Embankment to live with us, much to Birdy's amazement, if not amusement. Later in the eighties he came to our farmhouse in the country too and there, out of the Amsterdam atmosphere, he relaxed and became more like the old Bart we had known in the beginning. We would go for long walks and he would be endlessly interesting with his great knowledge of natural history. I remember one time in Morocco a rat appeared at the kitchen window. My reaction would have been to chase it off. Bart picked up a piece of cheese and, approaching softly, offered it to the rat. As it ate out if his hand he had a little conversation with it.

Once back in Amsterdam, however, the shutters would go up again. Amanda still kept on visiting him. He had got a job, through the Unemployment Office, working in the library of the Tropical Museum. It was a job he found tolerable, because it gave him the opportunity to further his research into whatever it was that was occupying his mind at the time. He studied the macrobiotic diet, for instance, and realised that the value of it lay partly in its totally organic nature, excluding all toxins of any kind, and also in the fact that by following it the individual could produce vitamin C in his own guts, the fomentation of the miso encouraging the growth of the bacterium *Lactobacillus acidophilus*. Ironically, he learnt that the inventor of the diet, Georges Ohsawa, who used to travel round the world holding in his fist a ball of brown rice wrapped in seaweed, the minimal daily survival diet, eat the local food until he contracted the disease indigenous to that area and then cure himself by going onto the macrobiotic diet, had died from lung cancer caused by smoking cigarettes!

Bart was allotted a council flat in a tower block in the most run down part of Amsterdam. He rode his bicycle to the library every day. For a time he had a hooker live with him for sex. He was surrounded by down and out Surinam junkies. Amanda visited him quite regularly. She said it was quite scary. All this time he was unrelenting in his insistence that the homework was the only way that the world was ever going to adopt his discoveries. It was like an overcoat which he pulled tight around himself to protect him from the cold.

One of his previous disciples, who had done his homework, joined the group, got trepanned and then left to return to America, was Peter Halvorsen. Twenty years later when Amanda and I helped an American filmmaker to do a film about trepanation, I suggested they find Peter to interview him. This brought him back into the picture. When he visited Amanda on his way to Amsterdam she asked him not to encourage the homework approach, as it had wasted over twenty years. He said he wouldn't, but once in Amsterdam he followed the homework path. By this time it was the nineties and the world wide web was established on the Internet. Bart saw that this was the opportunity to put his message down and make it permanently available. With Bart's help Peter built a website, www.trepan.com, and assumed the role of Mr Trepan, as Bart called him. Peter found a surgery in Mexico which was prepared to perform trepanations for a fee of $2,000 and advertised this fact on the website. In order to qualify for this the subject first had to do the homework. He did get a few takers, a handful at least, then ran into trouble.

Bart had held high hopes that putting the information out there on the Internet would at last produce the breakthrough. He told Peter that he would give it five years and if nothing had happened by then he would drink himself to death. Shades of Henk. This is exactly what he did. Arie told me that he used to drink two litres of Dutch gin a day, real gut rot. He shunned the company of humans. He said he preferred lizards. He was seventy-two when he died.

What went wrong? Why did Bart paint himself into a corner? Would it have made any difference if he hadn't chosen this route? Obviously I am biased, in that I did not like the cult atmosphere with its myopic self-centredness, its exclusive attitude to the rest of the world. But then I am a product of the affluent middle class of a developed country with a first class liberal education, born with, relatively speaking, a silver spoon in my mouth etc, as indeed was Bart. Bart could point out that he got more results his way than I ever did mine, but I was only trying to introduce people to Bart's teaching and, ideally, Bart himself. At this moment in time, as the Americans would say, there are perhaps thirty or forty people alive who have been trepanned as a result of Bart's teaching. Of those I have been partly responsible, directly or indirectly, for no more than four. But it must be remembered that Bart was the inspirational genius, the discoverer. Naturally people were attracted by his charisma. Why go to the disciple when you could go to the master? It was not my aim to have a lot of followers, rather to act as an advertising agent for Bart, and herein lay the difficulty. Amanda and I did everything we could to draw attention to Bart's teaching, but, from our perhaps privileged position, we became increasingly reluctant to refer journalists or other people to Bart, since the image presented by the cult was so low-level and unattractive as to prove counter-productive. As it happened, fortunately, the homework rule applied to journalists as much as anybody else, so they couldn't get to see Bart even if they wanted to. But one didn't want to have to tell them this!

Here was this dynamic, attractive, major personality, natural leader, shutting himself up in a cupboard and throwing away the key. The point is he would have attracted just as many followers if he hadn't made it into a cult, indeed in my opinion many more. Cults appeal only to a certain type, especially the weaker and more impoverished personalities, and individuals who have no wish to be subsumed within a group identity avoid them like the plague. Now there is an argument that this is a snobbish attitude and that it doesn't matter if the "army of truth" is composed of the *jeunesse dorée* or the scum of the earth. Once clad in the armour of righteousness, the warriors of peace and love attain nobility through the justice of their cause. If this is so, it is equally so whether they are members of a cult or not. It is not an argument for or against cults. Bart's argument was that it was the only way to make sure that the message was transmitted. The taboo was so strong in normal society that it was impossible for an individual to stand up against it. The isolation that resulted from banging your head against a brick wall would drive you into a self-imposed ostracism and madness. Only with the strength of the group behind you would you have the strength to brave the ridicule of the mob.

It is certainly true that having knowledge you wish to impart but cannot is isolating. To be the bearer of unrecognised truth is isolating. I have been fortunate that I have lived with people who do recognise the truth of the message, but then you choose your companions, don't you, unless you are in prison?

From that high point in 1966 there was a gradual descent to the tragic end. If he had been allowed back into the country and gone on living with Amanda I am sure that things would have developed in a completely different way. Having had the peach snatched from his hands, as it were, he went into a giant sulk. Iron entered his soul and he determined to punish the world for turning its back on him by turning his back on it. In his mind he was giving it a chance by holding out the homework hoop for the world to jump through, but in reality he was excluding himself from mainstream life and confining himself to a world where he was surrounded by intellectual inferiors and had no worthwhile feedback from his peers.

The psychedelic movement, if such a term can be applied, was the spreading of a new set of values derived from the high experience. It was the turning on of the world, first to marijuana, with the beatniks, and then to acid and other hallucinogens in the sixties. The instant enlightenment that was achieved through LSD was a very valuable experience. It could change the whole way you perceived the world. A lot of the older generation were scathing in their scornful attitude. Enlightenment, they said, is something you have to work towards over a lifetime. The truth in this is that wisdom does take time to grow, but this does not mean that the vision of acid, the mystical experience, takes a lifetime to grow. The vision is instantaneous, but it may take a lifetime to recreate the world inside your head to fit in with it, to rearrange your priorities in accordance with the "heavenly sphere". It is, of course, extremely irritating, to say the least, for those who have been labouring up the steep paths of meditation or prayer to be told that they could just as well take a pill, but they can rest assured that the wisdom they attain on their snail-like progress cannot be attained any other way. Whether they will ever achieve the vision of total consciousness at the end of their arduous journey is another question. I am not in a position to know, though I must say that I have the gravest doubts in most cases.

Within the psychedelic movement, the great current of consciousness which swept through the minds of the youth in the sixties, the waves of which have been surfed by succeeding generations, the overriding impulse is to simply enjoy the sensory experience of living, to revel in the expanded awareness of the senses which the increased blood in the brain brings with it. It is the transcendence of the Ego, the realisation that it is not the word but what it represents that is important, not the concept of the love of God, but the actual feeling of it. No amount of arguing about it in theological college, even over a lifetime, will ever compete with the direct experience of it. Once you have experienced it you realise it doesn't matter what you call it. You can call it what you like, that's not the point.

It's not the main point of the experience, the explanation, but at the same time it is a very important thing, because understanding what is happening not only provides the safety measures, to insure against insanity or flip-out, but also a reality check which can safeguard against irrational fantasies getting the upper hand. To use a mountaineering metaphor, the explanation of the experience which Bart provided is, in my opinion, an essential piece of equipment for scaling Mount Olympus. It is the guide book. Bart saw that the movement could result in madness and chaos if the drugs were taken in ignorance. The problem was that the vast majority of people did take them in ignorance, so the experience was spread, but the word never was. His attempts to bully the world into understanding were doomed from the start. That's not the way things go. A new truth, especially one as esoteric and complicated as this one, takes a long time to seep into consciousness. It is frustrating for those "in the know". Bart was impatient. Apart from anything else, he was human, and he wanted recognition for his work. Unfortunately his megalomaniac side misjudged the scale of the problem. To him the world was a little child, to be scolded into obedience. To the world he was a little child sulking in the corner.

Had he used his undoubted charisma on a bigger stage, in time he would have attracted the attention of more serious players and the information would have had an airing in a wider world than the medical profession. It would have reached the ears of those in more appropriate areas. As it was, Amanda and I, who would have made a formidable team with him in this endeavour, were left up a pole as the barge sailed on without us. He was the authority, we were his acolytes. Naturally people we talked to wanted to meet him. If we couldn't produce him it cast doubt on our role. If we had produced him it would have cast doubt on the whole matter. It would have been a turn-off rather than a turn-on. Bart, in his charming, quiet, humorous mode, with his knack of making memorable aphorisms, would have been a great attraction in the media. People would have flocked to listen to him; in the severe role of underground cult leader, quite the opposite.

All of this begs the question what made him take this extreme route. He was a perfectionist, an extremist in fact. Everything he did was carried through to the last detail. My none too original opinion is that it was his mother's death which was the determining event in his life. In overcoming it he managed to make use of the positive energy her love had bequeathed him, to sublimate his love for her into an almost obsessive passion for his subject, but the overcoming also demanded a severe repression of her memory, a negative energy which he later transferred to the exclusion of the world. He was, as I've already mentioned, a scientist to his fingertips. He didn't want to leave anything to chance, believing that there was a formula for everything; once you'd worked out the formula chance was excluded. Fate had dealt him one almighty blow and he was determined to leave nothing to chance if he could possibly help it.

After Richard Hubner's death, the cult aspect died down. Individuals who had been through the homework hoop left the group and were absorbed into the mainstream of life again.

I know a few, some nice, intelligent people, some alive, some dead. Bart withdrew even further, retreated into his cave, like Zarathustra. He maintained contact only with those who had done their homework, still excluding me even within that small group. He couldn't forgive us for being independent. Ironically, the foundation that he and Richard set up was called The Foundation of Independent Thinking. I occasionally wrote to him and got a letter back. Amanda still ventured occasionally into his lair in the housing estate. He studied things and wrote pieces about primitive people's way of living, arising from his study of the macrobiotic diet, and other pieces about the Tao.

He lived incredibly simply himself. He had absolutely no need or wish for the normal comforts of life. Eating was a scientific matter. You needed protein, vitamins, minerals etc. These minimal requirements could be provided by cooking brown rice once a week, having a few other basics in the flat and that was that.

What am I to say? It was my destiny to be his first disciple and I can only hope that perhaps now it is to be a sort of John the Baptist in retrospect and introduce him and his work to the wider world that he shut himself off from. It was a tragedy that he died in such a way. Was it unavoidable? It depends on how much of a fatalist you are. One thing is for sure. Things only happen the way they do – there is only one way. The illusion of choice is there, however. At each crossroads we exercise our free will and make a decision, do we not? If but one small detail was different then the whole picture might be completely changed – the beat of a butterfly's wings in Peking and all that. Well, it's over now. That's the way it went. But if Bart's life was tragic in its ending it was triumphant in its climax. His extraordinary knowledge and ability to express it simply and clearly were supreme, his humour and humility were the flip side of arrogance and contempt for small-mindedness.

Few men in history have been granted the privilege of seeing into the nature of things in such depth, of reaching into the white hot centre and pulling out such a diamond. The origin of the universe may be a tantalizing mirage leading inevitably to the old chicken-egg conundrum, but the evolution of the Ego has been revealed and in peeling off one more layer of the onion Bart has cast light into the darkest corners of the psyche and illuminated the internal landscape of man's mind.

Harold Macmillan once said that the only point of education was to tell when someone's talking rot. It is very useful to have the confidence in your own judgement to be able to do that. The possession of knowledge likewise has indirect benefits, in particular the removal of the fear that is engrained in ignorance. Ignorance of the facts of childbirth, that each contraction brings the end of labour a bit nearer, can make the pain seem unending and unendurable, whilst simply knowing that brings the comfort of realising that another obstacle has been negotiated and progress is being made. Similarly, knowing that a paranoia on LSD is a symptom of sugarlack draws the poison from the sting, so to speak, not to mention the fact that the remedy is apparent.

It is idle to speculate on what might have been had Bart not chosen the path he did, but from my point of view I feel sure that maintaining a friendship with Amanda and me would have been beneficial to him. I think at least it would have prevented him from running into a blind alley, a cul de sac. The companionship of people who were capable of constructive criticism could only have lightened the burden, made the game of breaking down the taboo more enjoyable. Amanda and I had always been ready to accommodate him in our life, so that he could spend time with Amanda and have a proper relationship with her as well as cooperating with me.

Bart had the mentality of a scientist. Everything could be reduced to a formula. He held, even clung, to the view that it was simply a matter of getting the information into the head and that the homework was the one and only way to do that. The problem with this approach is that it makes no allowance for humans being, in the words of Nietzsche, "all too human". Even scientists are human, even Bart was. Nobody is perfect, not even a God. (He had convinced himself that he had conquered jealousy when he was seventeen. He had done this by having three girlfriends at the same time, a method which revealed a blind spot of monumental proportions!) I always said that I thought it was more about personal influence. The point is that doing the homework was a ticket to Bart's company and it was his personal influence that people sought. That was why they were prepared to do the homework. In my opinion, with the right counsel, he could have had a far wider influence in his lifetime than he did. It is too late now, but it is not too late for me to sing his praises, to try and wake people up to what they have missed. If even a trace of his magic can be evoked by my writing then I will feel that the attempt has not been a waste of time. Over forty years ago I set out to be a writer. My journey led me to meeting Bart and finding a higher purpose, to bring news of his discoveries to the world. Only now, perhaps, can these two aims be reconciled if I can make use of the skill I have developed over the years to introduce one of the world's great unsung heroes to as wide an audience as possible.

IN CONCLUSION

It is now forty five years since I was trepanned, so I am able to look back and make some sort of judgement on the benefits of it. There are difficulties in doing so. For one thing I have nothing to compare it with. I can't tell what I would have been like without it. Still I can try to express what I perceive as the change.

The main advantage I am aware of is a mental resilience, a built-in bounceback, that I now take for granted. I remember the flatness that I felt in my early twenties, the feeling that I needed something to lift me off the floor, to make life more interesting, more exciting. It just didn't seem good enough to be confined to the monotony of a landscape without hills and valleys, or, to switch metaphors, to a worm's eye as opposed to a bird's eye view.

Since being trepanned I have never felt short of energy for the chores of everyday life. Of course I have my good days and bad, like everyone else; after all one can only play the cards one is dealt. But I feel a certain immunity to the slings and arrows, the buffets of the winds of fate. I feel a security in my identity, my inner being. I'm almost reluctant to write this, because I'm afraid of sounding like a snake-oil salesman. I don't want to overclaim. The outside world is full of sceptics. I do not expect to be believed. How much of this is down to a philosophical equanimity? Well, this is the point: I think that there is a physiological basis to it.

As a young man I was searching for the answer, an answer perhaps. I remember my wife, Jen, saying to me, soon after we met, that she was so pleased to find someone who wasn't searching. It struck me then that she was right. Since I learnt from Bart the materialistic explanation of expanded consciousness and found out for myself that, to quote Eve in *Paradise Lost*, "heaven is high, high and remote to see from thence distinct each thing on earth",

I do feel that I have found the answer. My problem is not to seek but to reveal.

To expand on the point about the equivalence of philosophical and physiological equanimity, it is necessary to bring in the importance of Bart's other discovery, the mechanism of repression and concentration in the brain, the Ego. For some unknown reason none of the many so-called experts in brain function have considered the blood supply as the most basic factor. It is of course a sine qua non, but as such it is so taken for granted that it is totally overlooked. That human beings repress is, I think, generally recognised. That we stand in the upright position is an undeniable fact. That this would have some effect on the blood in the brain is common sense. It is a hostage to gravity. What has been missed is the connection between the upright position and the consequent need for repression.

There were two big changes that occurred simultaneously in the mutation that produced homo sapiens erectus. There was an increase in the size of the brain and a prolongation of the growth period to almost twice that of our nearest primate cousins. Of course the adoption of the upright position had already occurred. The consequence that set us apart from all other animals was the development of the speech system. The increased brain size provided the space and the prolonged growth period the time for this, the space for the new centres to be formed in and the time for the meaning of the word to be established. By this I do not mean merely the most literal meaning of each word but rather the full development of the critical faculty, so that by the end of growth a person is potentially an independent thinker. Childhood is the dress rehearsal for the play of life.

That the human being depends on thinking for his survival is a statement of the obvious. That thinking depends on speech is equally non-controversial. That the speech system, that is the brain centres that comprise it, is the most recent of our major mental acquisitions, the latest to be established in the brain's evolution, is also an undisputed fact. Positioned as they are in the uppermost cortical layer, the speech centres are also the most vulnerable to the effects of gravity in the upright position. What Bart saw was that, because of this, a mechanism had evolved to ensure a continuous supply of blood to the speech centres. This is what he called the Ego and he saw that it was by means of constricting arteries leading to other parts of the brain, in other words by repressing function in those parts, that it maintained an adequate supply of blood to the speech system. First and foremost, function depends on a supply of blood.

What these insights forced Bart to realise was that, for all its advantages, the upright position brought with it one big disadvantage, a shortage of blood in the brain, which had been overcome only by the chronic repression of parts of the brain. I say chronic, because, since it is nature's way to take the line of least resistance, once a pattern of repression is laid down it tends to become set in its way and becomes characteristic to the particular individual, his character in fact. Some do it one way and some another. It depends on the personal history.

The sealing of the skull at the end of growth, the closing of the sutures between the plates, suppresses pulsation in the brain arteries and leaves us in a position of total dependence on the Ego for the maintenance of sanity, ie the correct functioning of the speech system. Without its repressing of other parts of the brain, the speech centres would be left high and dry. Since the key to the operation of this mechanism is recognition of the meaning of words – this is the stimulus for the reflex by which blood is concentrated in the speech centres; that is to say it is the recognition, by the listening centre, of the word spoken (silently in the case of thought) that causes more blood to be sent to the talking centre for the next word to be formed, and so on – it is not surprising that words and their meaning have assumed an importance in the life and history of man in comparison to which all else dwindles into insignificance. It is absolutely no exaggeration to say that it has been a matter of life and death. Religious wars have been fought over differences in interpretation between one sect and another, even when they share a belief in the same god, let alone when they believe in a different one, that is to say a different word. People will defend the particular meaning of their own words to the death. It is crazy.

The great beauty of getting high is that it transcends the Ego, it lifts one above the petty level of blind faith and intolerance to a place where one sees what we all have in common, irrespective of language. For me this has become a cause worth fighting for, because it is a struggle to get it across to the sceptical and disbelieving.

Can I explain how trepanation improves one's life? Only by repeating what I have already said over and over again. I remain as enthusiastic as I ever was about getting high and, with knowledge of the vital part played by the sugar level in functioning efficiently on the higher levels, I know that this can be done without danger of falling into confusion and ultimately insanity, the world of Humpty Dumpty. The fact that a crackpot or hole in the head protects the adult's speech centres from a state of bloodlessness was unknown until Bart discovered the reason for the operation having been performed all over the world since the stone age, the fact that the restored childhood level of capillary blood volume is high enough for the speech centres to "float" without need for the extra concentration provided by the Ego. In other words, with a hole in the head, even if your words do lose their meaning it doesn't mean that the speech centres will get no blood. When your sugar level is restored to normal your speech functions will be able to resume. I believe that, in order to continue to enjoy the high experience throughout life, trepanation is an essential foundation. It is not a great high in itself; it merely restores the brain metabolism to the youthful level it was at before the skull sealed, but that is a great bonus, an increase in energy for life and a platform from which one can take off like a bird and return to in safety. It provides the physiological equanimity that I spoke of.

Here is an observation that I am confident will meet with general agreement: there seems to be a universal feeling across the globe that adult life lacks a certain something. Why else do virtually all adults take measures to get high? Why can't they have a good time without taking drink or drugs or physical exercises designed to have the same effect? In all societies, from the most primitive to the most "advanced", people have worked out ways of putting more blood in the brain, or getting high. This surely is more than a coincidence; it is, rather, the indication of a need. Religions have been founded on the insights produced by these practices and rituals developed to hallow the incorporation of psychedelic substances.

Albert Hofmann was doing research with lysergic acid because of its exceptional vaso-constricting properties, which he thought could make it useful in obstetrics, to stop excessive bleeding. By accident he ingested some and the rest is psychedelic history. The width of the arteries is controlled by the central nervous system, which thus attempts to keep the blood flow as constant as possible in all circumstances, constricting or relaxing them as and when needed. The veins, however, have no nerves controlling them, so that any vaso-constricting substance in them will reduce their diameter. No research is needed to tell us that the effect of this is, inevitably, to cause the blood to dam up in the capillaries. Mere logic will suffice. In the brain this means that the capillary volume will increase, making blood available for millions of cells whose function is normally below the level at which it becomes conscious, or at which we become conscious of it. Every cell has a basic cell metabolism, which keeps it alive, but to function, to do its thing, it needs more blood bringing extra glucose and oxygen. This is what happens to millions of cells on LSD.

There really is no escaping this conclusion, which makes it all the more extraordinary that it has escaped the medical research establishment's notice, a classic case of not seeing the wood for the trees. As Shakespeare said, they miscall simple truth simplicity.

We only have one brain and much of its potential is untapped, due to a shortage of blood. Since it is the seat of all sensation, of insight, understanding, aesthetic appreciation, sympathy etc etc, it surely makes sense to unlock the untapped resources to make life a richer and deeper experience.

There are many drugs on the market these days and very little information about them. Education is essential and the most vital point of all is the difference between toxic and non-toxic drugs. Toxic drugs are addictive. They are poisons and the body produces anti-toxins to counter their effect, which leads to a craving for them on withdrawal. With frequent use you have to increase the dose to get the same effect. There are varying degrees of toxicity and addictiveness. Alcohol is toxic, but you can drink a lot without getting addicted, whereas heroin leads to addiction much more quickly. With toxic drugs there is a particular chemical effect which gives the drug its character, whether it be a stimulant, depressant, pain-killer or whatever. Many new designer drugs are produced with specific effects in mind and achieve their aims brilliantly. The problem with toxic drugs is that they have after and side effects, hangovers, comedowns etc, but the effects are so pleasurable while they last that, not surprisingly, users want to repeat the experience, especially since the effects are beneficial in some particular way that they value – alcohol loosens social inhibitions, amphetamines produce energy and a feelgood factor, heroin creates a sense of security and a "fuck you" attitude to the rest of the world. You only get these special effects with toxic drugs.

There are two dangers in taking drugs. The first is that many of them are highly toxic and can lead not only to addiction but also to damage of the organs, particularly the liver. Prometheus (the name means forethought or foresight) was punished for stealing fire from heaven by having his liver gnawed by an eagle for eternity. Gordon Wasson showed in his work that the fire was the sacred mushrooms. In primitive societies there is a legend that the mushrooms appear where the lightning has struck. It is well known that they come up after rain and some of them are very toxic.

The second danger is insanity and this comes more from taking the non-toxic drugs, particularly LSD. Marijuana is also non-toxic. Whilst it can create a psychological dependency, it is not physically addictive. LSD, however, is a special case. The amount one consumes is miniscule. Trips are measured in micrograms. A microgram is a millionth of a gram. 100 micrograms of LSD can fill the capillaries of the brain with enough blood to feed vast areas of the brain (billions of brain cells) that are normally starved, to bring the desert to life like the rains do. But this dose is too small to see with the naked eye. LSD is unique in this respect. All other drugs that get you high are measured in milligrams (thousandths of a gram) or grams. The danger is that, as the sugar level falls the meaning of the word gets weaker and weaker, the critical faculty gradually disappears until eventually the Ego is lost altogether. This is flip-out or psychosis. The importance of the Ego cannot be overestimated. The chain of word associations which normally keeps the speech centres active, in other words our thinking, is broken. The continuous supply of blood to the speech system cannot be maintained. Without it we are insane. We lose our sense of identity. It is astonishing how much glucose the brain can consume when all the braincells are firing simultaneously. It is hard for people to realise that there is an intrinsic connection between the bloodsugar level and the meaning of words. Our brains need the energy provided by glucose not only to articulate the words, but also to recognise or remember the meanings we have given them, we need it to focus our attention (concentrate the blood) on what we want to keep it trained on – without it our attention will wander all over the place and rather than riding the horse we will be taken for a ride.

The knowledge that a "high" is an increased volume of blood in the brain capillaries, or brainbloodvolume, with the logical consequence of sugarlack, which, when prolonged, leads to the loss of the word's meaning, the deconditioning of the conditioned reflex (Ego) by means of which blood is concentrated in the speech centres, throws new light on a lot of things, particularly the field of religion. It explains the paradox that Lucifer, the bringer of light, should be seen as the devil. In the Christian tradition all of man's problems are attributed to the weakness of Eve in succumbing to the evil serpent's temptation to taste the forbidden fruit and receive the knowledge of good and evil. Thus man was enticed to rise above his station and partake of the gods' psychedelics, which opened up the portals for his descent into the hell of insanity.

These dangers are very real, so it is not surprising that the bringer of light should have got a bad name. Witch doctors and witches have magical powers that terrify the good ordinary folk. Witchcraft was dangerous, taboo. Witches wore conical black hats to make themselves as invisible as possible when gathering the ergot off wheat by the light of the full moon, when the mould's ultra-violet reflection showed them where it was. From the ergot they obtained lysergic acid.

The ancient Greeks held initiation rites at Eleusis, at which the young men (women were not considered important in that patriarchal society) were introduced to psychedelics. The priests supervised events and kept things from getting out of control. But, whilst I would advocate the setting up of centres where the young could be taught the essential safety measures (sugar and vitamin

C) and inducted into the mysteries in a protected environment, the reality is that LSD is out there, available on the streets, and people are going to go on taking it in ignorance with the fateful consequences that are now well documented.

Unfortunately it has taken me many years to come to the conclusion that not everybody wants to know. Actually most people don't want to be told anything. It's like my mother's eldest sister, Judith. Joan, the second sister, was the clever clogs. She learnt how to read before Ju. When she asked Ju if she knew how to spell "cat", Ju said: "I don't know, I don't want to know, so please don't tell me!".

The drug problem is twofold: on the one hand there is the problem of addicts needing to maintain their habits by resorting to crime, so that they can pay the criminals who make vast profits peddling the drugs. This is the market for toxic drugs. On the other hand there is the problem of ignorant people taking non-toxic drugs and running the risks of insanity, caused by prolonged sugarlack, paranoia, the deconditioning of the Ego, the loss of the word's meaning.

All drugs that get you high do so by constricting the neck veins, which expands the volume of blood in the brain capillaries. That is what they all have in common. If this simple common factor was recognised I believe it would lead to a reassessment of the drug problem. Here is a research project for a chemist: list all the drugs that get you high and see if they all have vaso-constricting properties.

Human nature hasn't changed. The same emotions govern our behaviour as did when we were in caves, love, jealousy, greed and generosity. On the foundations of infantile bestiality we have built the towers of civilised behaviour, but when push comes to shove the beast bursts out like the Incredible Hulk and brings them crashing down. Can it ever change? If everybody was enlightened would it still be the same? We can dream, but is it realistic? I'm a born optimist, myself. We have the knowledge today. If we know how, we can take the right drugs and avoid addiction, organ damage and insanity. People like taking drugs and they are going to go on taking them, so let's make sure that the knowledge is spread. They like taking them because man needs to transcend the mundane level of adult life and let his spirit free, to be filled with love and wonder at the beauty of existence.

The old religions are dying. Their death spasms are in some cases extremely violent, but the course of social evolution is clear. Gradually a scientific and materialistic viewpoint is replacing the old metaphysical and metaphorical order. It's the same set of questions we are trying to answer, but our method has evolved from myth making to empiricism, from story-telling to scientific experiment. The possibility of enlightenment spreading beyond the inner circle to the general population is a real one, but it is only possible if the knowledge is spread with the drugs. I hope that this book may stimulate scientific research into the effects of changes in the volume of blood in the brain, both in totality for the expansion of consciousness and also locally for the distribution to the various brain centres under the control of the Ego. For over seventeen years Amanda has been working through the science programme of the Beckley Foundation trying to get answers to these questions, many of which are at the edge of, or beyond, the limits of what brain imaging can tell us.

So here am I, sitting here proclaiming this great new truth to the world and the world looks on wryly and says "but who are you to tell us all this? What are your qualifications? Are you a scientist? Are you a doctor?", to which I can only reply that I have nearly fifty years experience of taking psychedelics and I have found that the knowledge I'm teaching has enabled me to do this not only without harm, but also with great benefit both to my physical and mental health. The benefits are an abundant supply of energy, a depth and breadth of associations in the brain which provide the thinking with sounder foundations and general physical well-being through improved blood circulation all over the body. The one health problem I do have, which is the onset of type two diabetes in my late fifties – a genetic problem I share with my mother and brother – ironically provides me with a test and indeed a proof of the theory of sugarlack. Type two diabetes is not as serious as type one, for which insulin has to be injected at regular intervals. It is treated by diet and, in my case, half a tablet daily to aid insulin metabolism. It means cutting out excess sugar and fat from the diet. I have a portable blood-tester, which I use almost every morning to check the sugar level in my blood.

By trial and error I have found out what I can and cannot eat to keep it within bounds. I have found that when I take psychedelics I can indulge my taste for sweet things and still reduce the sugar level. If I take a trip at the weekend I will allow myself to have sugar in my coffee and eat normally forbidden delicacies, such as cakes or biscuits, and still keep the sugar level lower than normal. The same applies to alcohol (which incidentally has a very high sugar content itself, which makes the experience very positive and energy-giving to begin with, until it is used up). Professional advice is not to have more than two or three glasses of wine per day, which is what I usually have anyway. On occasions however, at a party, I will forget the restrictions and go for it. The result is always the same, a lower sugar level in the morning. My experience, therefore, proves that increasing the brainbloodvolume results in a lower bloodsugar level. I have tested this by taking a reading before taking acid and then taking another an hour or so after taking it, with the same result.

The orthodox scientific view on the action of psychoactive drugs is that they work by producing alterations in the function of neural transmitters, which can be observed in experiments. I do not contest these findings, but I think they are missing the bigger picture. Yes, the various toxic drugs do have chemical effects on the brain of course and it is these effects which make them attractive, but the "high" is one thing and the chemical effect is another. My contention is that the high is caused by an increased brainbloodvolume, due to constricted veins, and the special effects by the particular chemical action on the brain tissue. The bigger picture is that man suffers from a lack of blood in the brain due to the upright position and he seeks to correct this by taking drugs, frequently the most harmful ones. Drugs provide only a temporary relief from the predations of gravity. They increase the volume of blood in the brain capillaries. When the drug's effect is over the normal status quo is restored and we "come down". Nostalgia for the high state makes a repetition of the experience very attractive. Trepanation does not have the same effect as taking psychedelics. The change in the brain metabolism it produces, the "high", is hardly comparable. It doesn't cause a sugarlack, but it is a permanent rejuvenation.

Introducing Bart

Presented by Joe Mellen at Breaking Convention,
University of Greenwich, July 2015

The purpose of this talk is to introduce the work of a genius, Bart Huges, who has now passed away without recognition.

I met Bart in 1965, in Ibiza, right at the dawn of the psychedelic age. He was my teacher, or guru if you like. He was a scientist, a medical student, the son and grandson of doctors, when in 1962 he discovered the mechanism behind getting high and, a bit later, the secret of how repression is effected in the brain, something Freud had tried to explain in electrical terms in his "Project for a Scientific Psychology", a magnificent effort but ultimately, as he himself admitted, a failure.

Bart was first given LSD as a medical student in 1958, as part of a psychiatric experiment. He had hallucinations and saw one doctor as a devil with horns, another as a pig and a third as a chimpanzee. Six others saw the devil and three saw the pig. His wife Barbara was friends with a lot of people in the Bohemian stratum of society and gradually Bart moved into their company and started smoking pot. He soon became an enthusiastic smoker, since he had established that it was not toxic and wouldn't lead to addiction. He began to advocate it to his medical colleagues and when they had a daughter they called her Maria Juana.

In the sixties Amsterdam was the hub of the European smoking scene and their "happenings" were the precursors of the festivals that have subsequently become the main gatherings of the alternative lifestyle. It was at one of these events that took place in the Dam, the main square in Amsterdam, that Bart unfurled the ten metres of bandage that he had wrapped around his head after his trepanation, with HA HA HA… written in different coloured inks evenly spaced out along it. The joke was on gravity.

His advocacy of smoking marijuana had gained him a bad reputation in the medical profession. Furthermore, the police had raided his house looking for grass; it was reported in the newspapers which did nothing to improve his image in the profession. The top professor of psychiatry at the University of Amsterdam, who had previously asked him to become his assistant when he qualified, now told him that there would be no place for him to practise in the city. Bart's father had always told him that he regretted having practised medicine, because his patients never did what he recommended, to take exercise, be vegetarian etc, and if he had his time over he would have been a writer. Bart now decided to give up his career inside the profession and become an independent teacher on his own. His discoveries were not recognised by the profession. Indeed at that time, in the late fifties and early sixties, the very concept of expanded consciousness was unknown. It was not a subject that was studied. It did not fit into any of the categories in the syllabus.

Once free, the first thing he did, with another genius friend, a mathematician who had previously synthesised mescaline, was to make LSD. He got involved in a big hash deal to provide the funds for the various chemicals and the two of them made it in his friend's mother's house. At one stage in the process they used the bathtub and, while they were out having a coffee, the mother came in and took the plug out. This delayed the manufacture, since they had to re-acquire the lost chemicals, but eventually they succeeded. The acid was perfect. They dosed it out on sugarlumps. It was the first acid made in Europe outside the pharmaceutical companies.

Bart was, first and foremost, a biologist. He had always collected reptiles and amphibians. He would hitchhike around Europe on his holidays and catch snakes, lizards etc. He turned his bedroom into a terrarium. At one time he had over two hundred in his room, including a crocodile, which used to sunbathe on the branch of a tree that Bart had fixed sticking out of the window. He had caught it as a baby. When it had grown nearly to full size, the neighbours complained and he was forced to take it to the zoo. He would go there regularly to visit it.

He regarded man as the hairless talking ape, an animal like

all others, but with two peculiarities; first he stood upright and secondly he talked. Between them these two characteristics were responsible not only for the success of the species in evolutionary terms, but also for the perilous predicament it finds itself in. The invention of language has undoubtedly enabled Homo sapiens to achieve unparalleled technological and intellectual progress in both the physical and psychological spheres, gaining an understanding of the way things work, both inside and outside the body, but the flip side of the coin is that it has also led to the "tower of Babel" situation which bedevils our existence, the misunderstanding, suspicion and hostility which infect our relations with each other on the personal and international levels.

What Bart realised was that in adopting the upright position man was placing his brain at the mercy of gravity, which exerts its force on the volume of blood contained within the skull. This is a crucial point and no one before had ever considered it. There was a Eureka moment for Bart; just as Newton's moment was seeing the apple falling from the tree, for Bart the moment came when he saw Titi, an African yogi drummer, standing on his head at a party. When, after a considerable time, he stood up again Bart asked him why he had done that. "Well", said Titi, "if there's no weed to smoke I stand on my head to get high". Ah ha, thought Bart, I see I see, it must put more blood in the brain.

The upright posture, bipedalism, probably originated in apes around 4 million years ago. The most successful hominid species was Homo erectus, who lived from around 2m years ago until 500,000 years ago. They seem to have been the first to adopt the upright posture permanently. They were a social species, living in groups of around 20 to 50. They were the first to leave Africa and they used tools and/or weapons for hunting large animals and butchering them. They had also mastered fire and cooking. The demise of erectus coincided with the appearance of sapiens, and it is probable that it was the development of language that gave this new species the superior organisational ability to become dominant.

With the increased nutritional value available from cooking there was less need for laborious chewing and large guts. Smaller guts allowed for bigger brains, and there was one other characteristic that accompanied the evolution of sapiens – that was his increased growth period. This gave him the time for his speech system to mature, to master the ever-increasing vocabulary that he would depend on as an adult. Thus Homo sapiens gradually became the thinking ape, and with his mastery of language he was able to organise much larger social groups.

What Bart realised was that the speech system, which includes the centres for talking and listening, then subsequently reading and writing, was the latest to develop in the brain and of course these centres are in the cerebral cortex, the highest part of the brain, furthest away from the heart. In the event of a brain drain, the loss of blood from the brain due to gravity, their very existence would be threatened.

In every culture on earth there has been the myth of the Fall of Mankind, in the Judaeo-Christian world the expulsion from the Garden of Eden, which followed acquiring the knowledge of good and evil by eating the forbidden fruit. The fact that this myth is universal suggests that it is symbolic of something real. It is often explained in moral terms. In Greek mythology the Golden Age, in which man lived in peace and harmony, was followed by Ages denominated in diminishing values of metals, silver, bronze etc. What Bart revealed was that the Fall was nothing more nor less than the loss of blood from the brain due to the upright position, a loss further compounded by the sealing of the skull at the end of growth.

This is where we get into virgin scientific territory. Obviously everyone knows that the circulation of the blood is the most essential factor in life. Within the body whichever organs are in action attract a greater volume of blood than they have when not being used. When digesting a meal the stomach is engorged with blood; in the act of sex the sexual organs are, etc etc. The same thing happens in the brain. Whichever centres are in action attract extra blood. These are the basic facts.

The centres in the brain which require a constant supply of blood, however, at least in waking life, are the centres of the speech system, in particular the talking and listening centres, which we use continually in the act of thinking (talking to oneself under the breath). It is the recognition of the meaning of the word we speak in the listening centre that triggers the reflex to concentrate more blood in the talking centre, so that we can speak another word.

In this way a closed circuit between these two centres establishes and maintains priority in the distribution of blood to the speech system. Cogito ergo sum. This is what Bart called the Ego. It is a conditioned reflex mechanism.

He described how it actually works: the conditioned stimulus, like the ringing of the bell in Pavlov's famous experiment, is the recognition of the meaning of the word. The Ego is the organism's agent in the brain. It controls the distribution of blood in the following way; it is like the squeezing of a sponge. By constricting arteries leading elsewhere, it concentrates the blood in the centres in action. The constriction of the arteries leading to other centres that may want blood, because some perception or other has awakened them, results in the repression of their function. This is the basic mechanism of repression. It took a stroke of genius to see it.

So here is the situation we have. The speech system centres, high up in the cerebral cortex, demand the lion's share of the blood available in the brain. The fall of blood due to the upright position means that there is less blood available than in the four-legged position, with the neck horizontal. But there is one more factor that is relevant. When we are born the skull is in separate plates that fold over onto each other in the process of birth, so that they can emerge from the narrow passage of the cervix. The fontanels, gaps or holes, seal early in life, leaving the plates with sutures, or seams, of fibrous fingers between them. These seal very gradually in the course of growth, until at the end of that process, between the ages of eighteen and twenty one, they become completely ossified and the skull becomes a solid case around the brain, which is then no longer able to expand on the heartbeat, as every other organ in the body does. The pulsation of the blood vessels in the brain is suppressed. This results in a further loss of blood, since this pulsation had produced a pressure in the blood vessels which was exerted on the volume of water in the brain. It is not actually called water; it is called cerebrospinal fluid, but it is mainly water. This cerebrospinal fluid is produced in the brain and circulates only in the brain and spinal column. The central nervous system floats in it, as it were, and it protects it from the buffets of life. So when the sealing of the skull causes the suppression of the pulsepressure in the arteries and they consequently shrink, there is nothing to prevent the water from expanding its volume still further, which indeed it does, at the expense of the blood.

It is this further loss of brain blood at the onset of adulthood that marks the end of youth, and it is a bringdown. The natural spontaneity and creativity of youth diminish, and that is why we want to get high, to return to this youthful state of mind.

Bart consulted professional colleagues on ways of proving his hypothesis. The only objective method they could come up with was to mark the csf with radioactive isotopes, so that it could be traced and measured, but the amount required for this was considered too toxic and therefore impossible. So he devised seven different experiments, including physical tests, such as the headstand, chemical, taking non-toxic drugs, osmotical etc. Although the tests had to be carried out on oneself, the fact that they were repeatable by any individual fulfilled the scientific requirement for a proof. And after all only the subject can actually authenticate the expansion of consciousness. It can't be observed by anyone else.

He designed the exposition of these experiments in the form of a scroll, with the text flowing around a series of egg-shaped spaces containing schematic diagrams of the heart and brain, with the changes in the volumes of blood and cerebrospinal fluid depicted in each case. It was beautiful, a scientific treatise that was also a work of art.

Albert Hofmann was a chemist working for Sandoz when, unintentionally, he synthesised the most wonderful and purest psychedelic known to man, LSD. The reason he was working with lysergic acid was because of its strong vaso-constricting property. He was looking for something to help stop bleeding in childbirth. Strangely enough, after he had ingested some by accident, he didn't connect this property with the expanded consciousness he experienced. Bart, however, noticed that on acid the veins on the back of his hands were constricted and he put two and two together.

The circulation of the blood, in case anyone doesn't know this, consists of the blood being carried to the various organs in the arteries. It then flows into the capillaries, tiny hair-like vessels interfacing with the cells themselves, from which the exchange of nutrients (oxygen and glucose in the case of the brain) takes place, as does the discharge into them of the waste product of the metabolism, carbon dioxide. The blood is then transported in the veins back to the heart via the lungs, where the CO_2 is released into the air in exhaling and it is re-oxygenated in inhaling.

Now arteries have nerves attached to them, by means of which the central nervous system keeps the flow of blood constant. It can relax or constrict them for this purpose. So when a vaso-constricting substance is introduced it may result in an immediate reduction of blood flow, but ultimately the nervous system will relax its grip to maintain a constant flow. The veins, on the other hand, have no nerves attached. They are just drains. With a strong vaso-constrictor in them they will be strongly constricted, so less blood will be able to flow out through them. The inevitable consequence of this is that the capillaries will expand, so with LSD in the system the capillary volume in the brain will be greatly expanded, thus allowing millions, if not billions more cells to reach the level of metabolism at which their function becomes conscious – the threshold of consciousness. All cells receive some blood, enough to keep them alive at least, but whether their activity reaches this threshold depends on the volume in the capillaries and the level of metabolism that permits. The important thing to realise is that the vaso-constriction will be more pronounced in the veins than in the arteries, because the central nervous system will do everything in its power to counter the constriction of the arteries but can do nothing about the veins, so the effect will be relatively greater in them.

Bart did some research, which showed him that all drugs that get you high are vaso-constrictors to one degree or another. Of course many drugs are toxic and have their own characteristic chemical effects, which may be stimulant, narcotic or whatever. But the underlying cause of the high is the increase of blood in the capillaries. I'm not going to say that neuro-scientists and others who study drugs lose sight of this fact; the fact is they have never caught sight of it. They have never considered the physiological aspect of the matter. For them it is all a matter of chemistry.

The most powerful instrument at man's disposal is his imagination – it is an instrument which in the mind of genius has produced all the greatest discoveries and inventions in history – the instruments which he has made to measure and investigate the world around him are merely the means to validate the feats of imagination… for example William Harvey came up with the idea of the circulation of the blood and postulated the existence of capillaries in 1628, but this was not confirmed for many years, until microscopes powerful enough to prove it were invented. It was only in 1661 that Marcello Malpighi first saw capillaries.

In recent experiments neuro-scientists have been conducting, with volunteers on psychedelics undergoing fRMI scans, it is reported that one of the things they have observed is a reduction of blood flow to a part of the brain they call the DMN, Default Mode Network, the organising hub, or Ego. This is exactly what Bart's theory would predict, since the constant repression normally required to keep the speech centres supplied with blood is no longer needed, and maintaining that repression must take a lot of energy, or blood, and it would be the function of the DMN. I suspect that it is beyond the capability of the relatively primitive equipment available today (scanners etc) to see the constriction of arteries, let alone measure the volume of blood in the capillaries, but if their operators knew what they were looking for it would certainly make life easier.

Because there is a close similarity between the molecules of LSD and serotonin, this has lead neuro-scientists to propose that it is LSD's ability to mimic serotonin's role of neurotransmitter that is responsible for the mood-enhancing or depressing effects of the drug, and they need look no further for its action, but this is by no means conclusive. Of course if there are vastly more brain cells functioning at the conscious level of metabolism there will be more awareness of mood swings. The chicken of exaggerated moods, good or bad, will spring from the egg of increased capillary blood volume, with its consequent hypoglycaemic symptoms. By restricting their assumptions to this chemical perspective, they overlook the more basic fact of hypoglycaemia. The proof of that comes from the experience of taking sugar to counter the distorting effects of its symptoms.

What is consciousness? Well, whatever else you can say about it, what is incontrovertible is that it is a product of brain metabolism. It is energy, it is light. It is the awareness of what is taking place inside the organism and outside it. The brain metabolism is the oxidation of glucose. Glucose is created by photosynthesis, through the action of sunlight on plants. When consumed by man, as the sunlight encapsulated in the plant is oxidised, it is released as consciousness in the brain, so you could say that it is the shining of the sun in the brain. The more glucose that is oxidised the brighter the light.

What is important is the level of metabolism of a brain cell, or a cluster of brain cells – that is what decides whether the activity that takes place therein becomes conscious… a lot of action takes place without us becoming aware of it. In this case the neurotransmitters are still doing their job, messages are still being passed from cell to cell, but we are not aware of it. Whether we are aware of what is taking place in the braincells depends on the strength of the fire that is burning inside them – the burning question, as it were, is how bright is the light generated? Does it reach the level at which we notice it? Just as there is a range of frequencies that we can hear and a spectrum of wavelengths of light that we can see, so there is a level of brain metabolism that determines whether we are conscious of the activity taking place or not. Below a certain level we do not become conscious of it.

With a greatly increased volume of blood in the brain capillaries, the amount of glucose consumed by the brain increases exponentially. In normal adult life the brain, which makes up 2% of total body weight, consumes 20% of the total daily carbohydrate consumption. Since glucose is the sole source of energy for the brain, it actually accounts for 50% of daily glucose intake. On LSD the number of brain cells reaching the conscious level of metabolism is vastly expanded and consequently the glucose consumption is hugely increased too. This results in the hypoglycaemic symptoms so well known to occur; cold hands, chills, trembling, perceptual distortions, paranoia and hallucinations, not to mention the weakening of the meaning of the word, the loss of the critical faculty, which can result in the enormous inflation of significance to a few particular words. I have seen people in the throes of extreme sugarlack repeating phrases such as "today is tomorrow is yesterday is today is tomorrow is yesterday …" over and over endlessly as they cling to the last vestiges of their Egos. Eventually, as the sugar level continues to fall, even that will go and there will be no one at home in the head. Knock, knock – no answer. That is what we used to call flip-out, as opposed to freak-out, which is a temporary occurrence of some frightening episode.

With knowledge of the facts about sugarlack it is easy to take measures to escape a freak-out – it is a matter of taking sugar to restore sanity. Without the knowledge the experience can go from bad to worse. The sugar level is controlled by two hormones, adrenalin and insulin. When it gets too low adrenalin is secreted and glucose is injected into the blood from the liver. When it gets too high insulin is secreted, which extracts the surplus and stores it in the liver. For the synthesis of adrenalin, ascorbic acid (vitamin C) is essential. Incidentally, besides injecting glucose into the blood, adrenalin also constricts the veins, so in emergency one has a shot of the two things one needs most for optimal function, more blood and glucose in the brain. The body cannot store ascorbic acid, as it does other vitamins, and with the repeated use of adrenalin which comes with an acid sugarlack the body's supply can run out quite soon. It is therefore advisable to take a time-release vitamin C pill with a trip, or have fruit or another source of it available to take during the trip.

Because the use of adrenalin is usually triggered by fight, fright or flight situations, its use on acid because of sugarlack will often give rise to associations of that nature, leading to a chain of frightening images or feelings, known as "the horrors". Another thing to remember is that, ironically, on a low sugar level, the last thing you want is sugar. Nonetheless it is what you need to extricate yourself from the situation.

Freud gave the image of the Ego as the rider and the Id as the horse. When the Ego is lost the horse will take you anywhere it wants. If it decides that it wants to fly, there is nobody to say that it is impossible. With the distorted perspective of a sugarlack, to zip across from one side of the Grand Canyon to the other can appear like a doddle – just spread your wings and you will probably catch a thermal!

In the sixties, when acid first broke onto the scene – and standard trips were then 250mcg – many people thought that the sugarlack was the point of the experience. They vied with each other in describing their surreal adventures. Whilst I am not saying that it has no value, particularly in the regressive experience which can have psycho-analytic value, revealing repressed feelings and thoughts, and help in self-understanding, what I can say is that if you keep your bloodsugar at an adequate level to maintain your ability to concentrate and focus your attention where you want it, that is an altogether more positive and thrilling experience. The breadth of association which comes from the expanded consciousness is not lost; on the contrary it remains available for giving added depth to one's insight; the critical faculty is sharpened and one can come to conclusions with heightened vision and clarity of thought. With an adequate sugar level one's intellectual powers are enhanced.

So, let's recap: adult man depends on his Ego to maintain his sanity – that is because he depends on thinking and thinking is a function of the speech system, and the speech system depends on this mechanism of repression to keep it being supplied with blood. In other words, you could say that, as adults, we think at the expense of some degree of vitality, that is function repressed to keep the speech system active.

There is a general rule for all things to have a tendency to inertia, to take the line of least resistance. Just as water will flow down an already existing channel rather than forge a new one, so will blood in the brain. Once a pattern of repression has been established it is likely to become chronic. This explains how neurotic patterns get established in childhood and remain fixated later, despite the original reason for the repression – some parental prohibition or infantile trauma for example – having ceased to have any relevance today. The behaviour, however, has become permanently deviated. It is for this reason that psychedelics can be valuable in a psycho-analytic sense, since with an increased capillary blood volume the speech system no longer depends on the pattern of repression that normally sustains it, and those complexes can be allowed an airing. In the light of reason they may be seen for what they are, relics of early traumas that have no relevance today. An image that I think conveys the situation rather well is that of an oil rig in the North Sea. The platform is anchored to the sea bed by steel legs. Likewise the Ego puts down roots into the psyche and these roots are chronically constricted arteries, so that the whole thing becomes an immovable structure instead of a flexible ad hoc arrangement. Some repression is necessary to keep the speech system functioning, but it doesn't HAVE to be a chronic pattern laid down in childhood.

Just to give you an idea of the strength of the Ego's repression I will tell you a story about my childhood. I was an avid reader and I was sitting in the nursery, reading with my back to a fender in front of an electric fire. Suddenly the door burst open and my mother rushed into the room. I looked up and saw the whole room was full of smoke. The back of my jersey was charred black. I was so engrossed in the book that I hadn't noticed a thing. I'd repressed all the obvious warning signs in order to keep reading!

Repression gets a bad name in some quarters, but it is an essential action in life. When the mouse sees or smells the cat he will leave the cheese. He'll repress the urge to eat for the sake of survival. When you're about to step into the street and you suddenly see a car approaching fast, you repress the action of stepping, for the same reason. It's just saying NO.

In the case of the Ego, the repression needed for its maintenance is not good for the general health of the organism. Any animal can perform all the natural actions it is capable of without any problem. For instance a bird can reach the root of every feather in its body with its beak. Compare that with the difficulty many adults have in touching their toes. Because of the scarcity of blood in the brain, homo sapiens erectus is in some respects sub-animal. Thanks to his Ego he can live in a dream world of his own making, far divorced from reality.

By the same token, however, increasing the blood volume in the capillaries by taking psychedelics is good for the general health of the organism. The action of the drug works its magic in the body as well as the brain. All the organs in the body benefit from this, improving their functions. One can run and jump faster and higher on acid than without it.

I used to play village cricket and I once went out to open the batting on acid with a glucose tablet in my mouth. The opening bowler was very fast. I had absolutely no fear and was able to play easily. I was out, caught on the boundary hitting a six! Oh well... can't win 'em all.

The problem with any measures one can take to counter the effect of gravity in the upright position is that they are only temporary. What goes up must come down. The increased capillary volume will only last as long as the drug's vaso-constriction lasts. In the case of acid it is probably three or four hours and then, when the effect stops, the previous status quo will eventually be restored as you gradually come down.

When thinking about the situation, Bart realised that there was one measure he could take that would be permanent, and that was to reverse the effect of the sealing of the skull by trepanation. Making a hole in the skull would enable the brain, as an organ, to reverberate again on the heartbeat. He knew that, anatomically speaking, the skull has a different origin from the other bones in the skeleton and that holes in it do not seal. The hole would allow the membranes around the brain to expand with the heartbeat and this would reintroduce the pulsepressure lost when it sealed.

He went to the leading brain physiologist in Amsterdam and explained what he had concluded, hoping to persuade him to arrange for him to be trepanned. The professor was sceptical and said anyhow he had measured the pulsation in the adult's skull. Yes, said Bart, by sticking a hollow needle through it! The professor was not for budging, however, so Bart realised he would have to do it himself.

The high from a hole in the head is no more than a gentle lift. If you call an acid high 100 and, say, a good hash 60, then the hole would be no more than 30. What it does, however, that is extremely valuable, is relieve the Ego from the need for chronic repression. The speech system can float again, as in childhood.

In 1970, after a few bosh shots, which are described in my book *Bore Hole*, I trepanned myself. Originally I used a hand trepan, something like a corkscrew but with a ring of teeth at the bottom of the shaft. It was an awkward procedure, a bit like trying to uncork a bottle from inside it, and it was unsuccessful. Subsequently I used an electric drill, which was much easier. It was comparatively simple.

I was alone in the flat, so when it was done I busied myself with clearing up the room and then waited to see if anything happened. In the next three or four hours the feeling I had was one of increasing lightness, literally as if a weight was being lifted from my mind. I began to notice it probably an hour after I'd finished the operation, and then it grew stronger. I hadn't really known what to expect and it was rather exhilarating feeling this gradual lightening. Would it last? Well, it remained with me till I went to sleep, and the next morning I was amazed to find that the feeling of lightness was still there. I hadn't come down. And in the days that followed I realised that it was a permanent change in my consciousness that had taken place. I was in a better place, ready for anything.

I always found the worst part of the coming down from a trip was the last part, when the heaviness of the old familiar adult routine set in again. After trepanation that is the part that you don't have – you stay just above that. I have to say that it is well worth it, and I am eternally grateful to Bart for showing me the way.

HOMO SAPIENS CORRECTUS

The Fall of Mankind:

I. Man's position is upright. II. The cranium seals at the end of growth. III. Blood is heavier than cerebro- spinal fluid. These three fac- tors cause the brainblood- volume to decrease as a mouth- ful of cerebro- spinal fluid re- places id. The brainme- tabolism slows down, originality and creativity diminish, youth has come to an end.

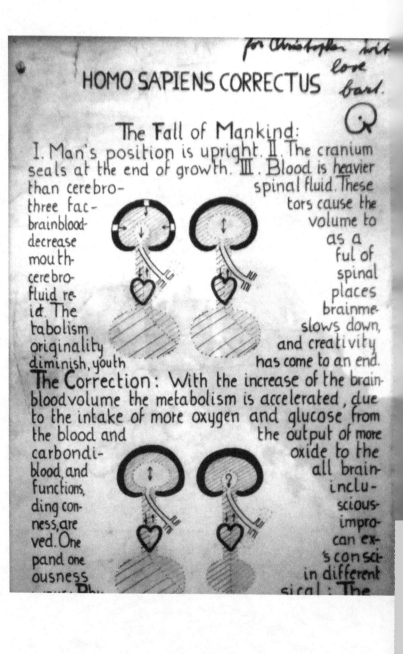

The Correction:

With the increase of the brainbloodvolume the metabolism is accelerated, due to the intake of more oxygen and glucose from the blood and the output of more carbondi- oxide to the blood, and all brain- functions, inclu- ding con- scious- ness, are impro- ved. One can ex- pand one s con sci- ousness in different ... Phy... sical: The

Bart Huges questioned by Joe Mellen
(Published in the *Transatlantic Review*, 1966)

M: You were born on the 21st of April 1934. Your father was a doctor, as his before him. Your mother died when you were two and a half years old. When Holland was occupied by the Nazis you were six. What are your memories of the war?

H: Well, individually I had a good time, as children do. I remember the hunger and the disappearance of Jewish friends, and once the Germans came to arrest my father because, like most doctors, he had refused to become a member of their "Kulturkammer". I remember seeing my grandfather at the end of the war. He had oedema of the legs caused by lack of protein – they were puffed up with water. He was completely starved. At the age of 85 he had been eating grass and leaves from the wood behind his house. That was all there was to eat. Liberation meant food – different uniforms in the streets, handing out chocolates to the children.

M: At school what were your main interests?

H: I had many interests: girls – I had 25 girlfriends when I was eleven; marbles – in the last year of the war I won a lot of money at marbles, selling back those I'd won and buying ice creams for my girlfriends. I also had many animals, mainly reptiles and amphibians. At eleven I had fifty snakes, lizards, toads, frogs, newts etc. At eighteen the number was three hundred and eighty five – that's the most I've had at the same time. I was fond of drawing and painting in watercolours, and after fourteen I spent more time on my homework, had one girlfriend and played table tennis and chess.

The last three years at school (from seventeen to twenty) were boring. I slept through the classes, waiting for them to end. At that time I read a lot, mainly philosophy – Plato, Nietzsche, Freud, Pavlov, Hesse etc. My interest in reading was awakened by Henk, who gave me a course of books to read. He was the only adult with whom I had contact and my confidence in them was badly shaken when he committed suicide.

M: On leaving school you started your medical studies. Why did you decide to do that?

H: My original idea, as a child, to study biology, developed into a study of the hairless talking ape. I wanted to specialise in psychiatry and psychoanalysis and then teach the subject.

M: When did you first take LSD?

H: In 1958, as a subject in a series of psychiatric experiments at the Psychiatric Department of the University Hospital in Amsterdam.

M: Did you take sugar?

H: No, because I hadn't discovered the mechanism then. I thought all sugarlack symptoms were essential parts of the experience.

M: Did you enjoy it?

H: Yes, though at the end I was very scared by the visual distortions (caused by sugarlack). I saw three of the doctors as a devil with horns, a pig and a chimpanzee. Six others saw the devil and three saw the pig.

M: In 1960 you got married on 15th March and then continued your studies. Did you have any more LSD experiences?

H: Yes, both Barbara and I had one more experience. We both enjoyed it.

M: Did you finish your medical studies?

M: Yes, in 1962 I took the main part of the doctor's exam (semi-arts), including psychiatry, neurology and pharmacology, and passed it. The second part (obstetrics and surgery) I took in April 1964 and failed in a theoretical part of the obstetrics exam. I took it again in front of the same doctor (it was the final part I failed – a ten minute oral exam in private with one doctor) and failed again. After that the government withdrew my grant, so I decided to forget it.

M: After ten years of study?

H: Yes. I did not want to practice medicine anyway. The restrictions imposed on doctors by the profession make it intolerable.

M: When did you first smoke pot?

H: All my friends smoked and had tried unsuccessfully to turn me on, but in the summer of 1962, after I'd passed the semi-arts exam, I went on a holiday to Ibiza to find out for myself if pot had similar effects to LSD and to see if it had any addictive qualities. In all the books I'd read it appeared as a non-toxic substance. I smoked as much as I could for a while and then suddenly stopped. Noticing no withdrawal symptoms, I then started smoking again.

M: In January 1963 you had a daughter whom you name Maria Juana. What were the reactions to that?

H: All sorts of hysterical nonsense. There were photographs of her in scandal articles, associations with orgies, declarations that my wife and I were not married etc etc.

M: In November 1962 you discovered the mechanism of brainbloodvolume. What led to the discovery?

H: Having got high from smoking pot in Ibiza, I met Titi there. He used to stand on his head at parties for considerable periods of time. When I asked him why he did it, he said it got him high. My father stood on his head every morning – to "keep fit", he said. I had always felt fit anyhow, so had seen no reason to adopt the practice myself. But now I stood on my head for a quarter of an hour and got high. In November, in Amsterdam, Germ (who has the third eye from a car accident and who named his daughter Mescalinea) gave me some mescaline, and it was then that I got my first clear picture of the mechanism, realising that it was the increase in the volume of brainblood that gave the expanded consciousness. An improvement of function must have been caused by more blood in the brain, which meant there must have been less of something else. Then I realised that it must be the volume of cerebrospinal fluid that was decreased.

M: What was the medical explanation of it at that time?

H: An unknown chemical action on the brain cells.

M: How did you discover the action?

H: Although I was aware of the effect of the action – to increase the brainbloodvolume – at that time I hadn't perceived the action itself, the constriction of the veins. I perceived that later, on LSD.

M: So once you had discovered that expanded consciousness was caused by an increase in the brainbloodvolume, it was a logical step to the need for sugar with LSD etc?

H: Yes. That brain cells take more glucose from the blood than body cells do is common knowledge in the medical profession.

M: Sugarlack is inevitable if you increase your brainbloodvolume?

H: Yes. The brain lives on glucose and oxygen, whatever anyone says about the holy ghost and spiritual bread.

M: When did you decide to have the "third eye"?

H: In prison, having checked the mechanism by perceiving the warm cerebrospinal fluid in the back outside the central nervous system (after using the pressing-up method described in the scroll), I thought about making a hole at the base of the spinal column to let the fluid out and, while thinking about holes, I realised that pressure was necessary to squeeze the fluid out of the system. Then, having concluded upon the nil pressure inside the adult skull (in most adults the skull seals between the ages of eighteen and twenty-two) I saw that any hole in the spine would heal over, so it had to be in the skull, where holes stay open.

M: Once you had decided to have the "third eye", what did you do?

H: One of the main reasons I wrote the scroll was to give the knowledge to the doctors. I visited about twenty professors, of psychiatry, anthropology, neuro-anatomy etc and their reactions were without exception negative.

M: What do you mean "negative"?

H: They were polite but uncooperative. Two surgeons said they understood the mechanism but dared not even ask their superiors for permission to perform the operation.

M: For how long did you try to find a doctor to do it before deciding to do it yourself?

H: For two years.

M: Then on Jan 6th 1965, despairing of assistance from the medical profession, you operated on yourself?

H: I had planned to do it six months earlier, but my friends took away my tools and prevented me from operating.

M: So you had to conceal you intention the second time?

H: Yes. My wife knew I was going to do it, but no one knew when.

M: What tools did you use?

H: An electric drill, a surgical knife and a hypodermic syringe for the local anaesthetic.

M: How long did the operation take?

H: Three quarters of an hour.

M: Was there any pain?

H: No.

M: Not even afterwards?

H: No.

M: How long was it before the wound healed?

H: Three days.

M: What was the first effect you noticed?

H: The appearance of pressure inside the skull. It took about four hours for the cerebrospinal fluid to be pressed out.

M: And now you are permanently high. How would you describe your state to someone who has never taken consciousness-expanding drugs or stood on his head for quarter of an hour?

H: I feel as I felt before the age of fourteen.

M: If you are permanently high now, aren't you on a permanent sugarlack?

H: The sugar-level in my blood is lower than it was, but the liver and adrenal glands have adapted to the greater need for glucose.

M: What happened after the operation?

H: I made it public ten days later by having the bandage removed at a happening. A week later I gave a press conference, before which I went to the University Hospital to have an x-ray photograph taken. I was detained for an hour by two psychiatrists and released only when I promised to return the following day. I told the journalists this, but they didn't mention it in the papers. The next day I went back with two witnesses. Then ten male nurses formed a circle around me and forced me into the clinic, where I was kept involuntarily for three weeks for "observation". The day after my release the news was announced in the press. A month later I made a television appearance, soon after which the government issued a statement – read out in the television news – to the effect that Bart Huges's scroll "Homo Sapiens Correctus" was not 99% but 100% nonsense!

M: Do you advocate the "third eye" for everyone?

H: I advocate the availability of trepanation for every adult who wants it.

M: Who will want it?

H: Everyone who understands the mechanism. There is no reason why a single adult should be left behind if he wants to be liberated from gravity's drag.

M: What you're saying is give the adult back his lost brainbloodvolume and he will look after himself, is that right?

H: Yes, with enough blood your central nervous system is a better doctor than your doctor.

M: What about diet?

H: Eat a salad every day.

M: Do you think the adult state can have any advantage over the trepanned state?

H: No. The older one is the more will trepanation increase the benefits of experience.

M: You have said that social reform must start with the individual. Can you expand on that?

H: Gravity is the enemy. The adult is its victim. My problem is how to explain to the adult that he has too little blood in his brain to understand, if he has too little blood in his brain to understand that.

M: Do you think trepanned he can create a better social system?

H: I think no construction of adults can work optimally unless each adult in the construction is trepanned.

M: Do you foresee many changes in a trepanned society?

H: Increased efficiency in social operations, the restriction of activity to the essential and, with the restoration of originality and creativity to the adult, rapid progress in technology.

M: Do you see a future for art?

H: With a rejuvenated adult art is likely to become a common activity – no longer an "in" commercial enterprise.

M: You have been accused of coming as a Messiah. What do you think of that?

H: I do really prefer my trepanned state to my previous adult state, but I am an atheist and certainly not sent by anyone.

M: Do you think LSD should be available to the general public?

H: Only with sugar (1 pound per trip) and extra vitamin C, and in supervised centres. Supervision by those who understand the mechanism is necessary to prevent people from falling the victims of their own ignorance.

M: Your view is optimistic, but can you be sure that in a trepanned society the particular interests of the individuals will complement each other? Might it not be merely an acceleration of chaos and conflict?

H: I am sure that an increase in common sense will result in an increase of cooperation. There will be less conflict and chaos because communication will depend less on the number of words and more on their meaning.

M: There is a lot of talk among our wilder visionaries about a change in the modes of communication, the substitution of colours for words for example. How about that?

H: I think it's a good idea to exchange the unnecessary words for colours and keep the few left for the communication of information.

M: In the state you predict what part will be played by women?

H: Trepanation will bring everyone to a better realisation of their potentialities. In my opinion the potential functions of the central nervous system are identical in male and female.

M: Do you think man can now live without religion?

H: Trepanned man will not find it necessary to give meanings to abstract words or to invent new superstitions. "Faith in the immortality of the soul" is a chain of associated meaningless words.

M: Is there any hope of something replacing fear as the motive impulse behind behaviour?

H: Gravity is the enemy. A large part of adult behaviour is motivated by the fear of losing the grip on what blood is left in the brain. Trepanation, by restoring the blood lost in the course of growth, removes the main cause of fear.

M: In a trepanned society there will be more individuality and independence than in the present one. What part do you see the state playing?

H: I think the state should serve the individuals, not vice versa. It should provide all the essential needs.

M: How do you explain the turning to eastern doctrines and religions which the use of LSD has brought in America?

H: It is a reaction to the apparent chaos of western civilisation

– but they don't understand the mechanism, so they don't take sugar. I can understand them looking elsewhere than in America, seeking the secret in the esoteric doctrines of ancient religions – but of course there is no secret.

M: Do you think the mechanism has been known before?

H: There are no signs that the mechanism itself has been known, though facts connected with it, around it, have been known – for instance yoga headstands and trepanation have always been practiced.

M: They knew the effect, but not the cause?

H: If they did know the mechanism the knowledge was never recorded.

M: Has trepanation been used as the cure for insanity before?

H: Yes, it is described as such in the painting and writing of Hieronymus Bosch.

M: Why do you think the practice has died out?

H: It must have got an undesirable reputation because it was known as a cure for insanity. It was probably regarded as a stigma showing that the bearer had been insane.

M: But it has never, to your knowledge, been used for other reasons?

H: Not on a large scale. Certain ancient civilisations used it, and it has been and still is a religious practice in some parts of the world. In central Africa it is used commonly for the treatment of various diseases.

M: The established Western view of the operation is that it constitutes mutilation, that it has no indication?

H: Yes. The mechanism is unknown to the medical profession. In fact there are two indications: the general one is adulthood, the particular one insanity.

M: Adulthood is hardly a disease, is it?

H: It is the end of youth, an unnecessary handicap. Whether you call the loss of brainblood to gravity a disease or not is irrelevant – it is certainly a loss, which can be recovered.

M: Is there any contra-indication?

H: No. I suppose in cases of severe adulthood there might be a depression immediately after the operation in a period of retrospection.

M: How did you come to the realisation that the Ego is a conditioned reflex?

H: From the observation that other people's Egos were deconditioned by prolonged sugarlack I concluded that the Ego is a conditioned reflex.

M: What was it thought to be before?

H: Freud gives it a place among the parts of the personality, but does not define it. Descartes said "cogito ergo sum", and Sartre had some thoughts about it – I forget what they were.

M: You have been quoted in the newspapers as saying that anyone can easily trepan himself. Is this your opinion?

H: In the scroll I have written "with today's knowledge of operating techniques one can easily do this by oneself...". I have not written "without today's knowledge..." because I did not mean that.

M: One last question. What is your definition of genius?

H: Someone born with knowledge of the difference between no and yes.

The Hole Story of My Life

Jenny Gathorne-Hardy

Published in *The Independent On Sunday,* 17 September 1995.

IT WAS a quick decision to get trepanned. I met Joe Mellen a year ago and my first thought on meeting him was how very normal he seemed. I was taken aback, for normality and drilling a hole in one's head are not as a rule associated. It was this very ordinariness that prompted me to question him on the quite horrific-sounding operation he and his former partner Amanda Feilding had performed on themselves almost 30 years ago. He told me that with a special drill used in surgical operations he had drilled a hole of approximately six millimetres in diameter through his skull to allow the brain to pulsate again. Grimacing, I asked if it had been painful. "Not at all," he said.

I didn't relish the thought of his DIY surgery, to put it mildly, and if it hadn't been for something about him I would have refrained from taking the subject any further. All the while he had been speaking, however, I'd become more and more aware of a kind of energy in him, a vitality and freshness one normally associates with youth – not with a 56-year-old man. There was a clearness in his eyes and he exuded a sort of lightness that I've rarely seen in an adult before. It was for these reasons that my attention remained held. I wondered if trepanation could have any bearing on these attributes.

He certainly thinks so. He believes the theory that the sealing of the sutures in the skull at around the ages of 18 to 21 prevents the brain from pulsating with the heartbeat. With this the ability of the blood to reach to topmost part of the brain – the outer cortex, used to speak and think and give meaning to the world – diminishes. Suddenly, unlike in childhood, the only way to keep the blood up there is by thinking. If we stopped thinking and lost this language centre we would be incapacitated. Life would have no meaning and we would have no memory of how to survive it. This is a terrifying thought and the human being is clever enough to prevent it from happening. He continually ensures a considerable amount of energy is used for and remains available for thinking. This, in turn, robs him of that energy he once had for other things and at the same time prevents him from relaxing with such ease. The need to keep thinking is a continual source of stress.

Over the next few meetings with Joe I became more and more intrigued. Finally, I felt the only way to test the theory would be to get trepanned. I can see that this might seem an extremely reckless move, to say the least, but he was talking about something I could identify with completely – the pressure of constant thinking, the familiar mental fatigue that accompanied me through each day, a general feeling that life was pretty much an uphill struggle. And the trepanationists were giving a reason for it that made absolute sense, saying too that the condition could be relieved in a matter of minutes. I talked in detail about the operation and could see how simple it was, but I certainly hadn't the courage (some would say foolhardiness) to perform it on myself. I find it difficult enough removing a thorn from my foot, let alone a drill from my head.

Since no doctor would do it, I asked Joe if he would consider trepanning me. He declined, saying his function was to teach it, not to do it.

I was undeterred. In a few days I had thought of somebody else who might do it for me, an old friend whom I felt sure would be attracted to the idea. I'd not seen Dave for years but something brought him to mind. Amazingly, after meeting Joe and talking at length to him about the concept, and about the operation itself, he agreed to trepan me. It was an extraordinary act of courage for which I am forever grateful.

The week before was devoted to buying the necessary equipment. Trepanning is done with a special surgical drill designed to prevent penetration of soft tissue once through the skull. By Thursday we had bought everything we needed. The only thing left was for Dave to practise with the drill. Someone had given him an old human skull to use, so with Joe's assistance he was able to become completely familiar with the procedure. On the Friday evening everything was prepared and ready for the following day.

While Dave practised on the skull, I bleached and arranged the room we'd decided to use. By the end of the evening it looked like a Victorian operating theatre. A table, strong enough for me to lie on, was cushioned and covered in clean sheets. A table next to it was also covered in a white sheet and held the surgical equipment: scalpel, syringe, bottles of sterilising fluid, metal trays, etc. In the middle of the table sat the skull Dave had been using. It became more and more like a scene out of Frankenstein, and although tension was mounting, we couldn't help seeing the funny side of it.

The three of us met the following morning. Neither Dave nor I was able to look at one another: I didn't want to acknowledge the fear in his eyes reflecting my own fear. We changed into a spare, clean set of clothes. Joe and Dave kept their hair back with transparent shower caps, rather uncomfortably adding to the surreal quality of the scene. After much washing of hands and arms Dave shaved a patch of hair about the size of a 50p piece from my head and bandaged the rest to keep the hair away. When he'd finished I looked like a boiled egg waiting to be eaten.

Suddenly I felt the most tremendous wave of terror. As the three of us entered our sterilised operating theatre, Dave and Joe in their shower caps and surgical gloves, and the skull on the table, I remember thinking: "I am in the hands of two madmen. Joe is a psychopath and Dave is simply a murderer." I lay down on the bed and each of them gave my hand a last reassuring squeeze. I closed my eyes. Dave was preparing the local anaesthetic and I was imagining Christopher Lee appearing at the door, holding in one hand the drill and in the other a brain in a jar marked "Abnormal".

I needn't have worried. The operation could not have been easier or quicker or more painless. Once the area had been anaesthetised it was a short while before it felt completely numb. There was absolutely no pain as the drill went through; the only discomfort was the loud noise resounding in my ears. The strangest feeling came from sensing the drill coming towards me as it moved through my skull; it was almost as if I was watching it. Simultaneously I had the clearest sensation that "I" is something inside my brain, not part of my skull at all.

Although the speed of the drill was kept extremely low, it was a short time before Dave was through. He removed the drill immediately and Joe came over to check and confirmed that he had done it. The drilling had taken little more than three minutes. The procedure had been as simple as we'd been told, proving to Dave and me that penetration of the brain had been an unnecessary fear.

I was lying on the bed and listening to the silence. The sun shone brightly through the window behind me. I couldn't believe it was all over. Tension had evaporated: there was just gentle murmuring from Dave and Joe as the wound was dressed and the old bandages removed. "There you are," Dave said, "all finished." I could feel him smiling.

Ten minutes later we'd cleaned and cleared up. Feelings of elation and relief filled the flat. A friend turned up and said it felt as though something had been set free. I was making tea for everyone and rapidly tidying up. I felt energetic and light. I don't know at this point if this was due to the hole in my skull or solely a result of the tremendous relief. Either way I was feeling extremely well and strangely buoyant.

Over the next few hours I began to feel a subtle but distinct change. It was as though for years I'd been a puppet with my head hung down, and now the puppeteer had taken hold of my head string and was gently pulling it up again. I felt a clarity and a gradual boosting of energy that didn't leave or diminish as time went by. I expected, and was waiting for, a mental "drop", but it never came.

In four days the wound had healed and on the fifth day I was on a plane to Thailand, a hair clip strategically pinned to the right side of my head. By the seventh day I was swimming in the sea and the memory of the week before was becoming more and more a surreal dream.

Three months later, the energy and clarity remain. I feel calmer and that particular mental exhaustion I became so used to has gone.

There is only one other person I have met with a stamina similar in quality to Joe's. It turns out that he, like a small percentage of the population, has a metopic skull, that is a skull in which the sutures never seal. Isn't it time research was done into the subject?!

List of Illustrations

Cover drawing by Amanda Feilding.

STRANGE ATTRACTOR PRESS 2023

Printed in the United States
by Baker & Taylor Publisher Services